SUNZI SPEAKS

THE ART OF WAR

Adapted and Illustrated by Tsai Chih Chung
Translated by Brian Bruya

Anchor Books
DOUBLEDAY
New York London Toronto Sydney Auckland

AN ANCHOR BOOK
PUBLISHED BY DOUBLEDAY
a division of Bantam Doubleday Dell Publishing Group, Inc.
1540 Broadway, New York, New York 10036

ANCHOR BOOKS, DOUBLEDAY, and the portrayal of an anchor
are trademarks of Doubleday,
a division of Bantam Doubleday Dell Publishing Group, Inc

Calligraphy by Wayne Truman

Library of Congress Cataloging-in-Publication Data
Ts'ai, Chih-chung, 1948–
[Ping hsüeh ti hsien chih. English]
Sunzi speaks : the art of war / adapted and illustrated by Tsai
Chih Chung ; translated by Brian Bruya. — 1st Anchor Books ed.
p. cm.
1. Sun-tzu, 6th cent. B.C. Sun-tzu ping fa—Illustrations.
2. Military art and science. I. Bruya, Brian, 1966–
II. Title.
U101.S96T7913 1994
355.02—dc20 93-40994
CIP

Table of Contents

Translator's Preface

The mere novelty of an illustrated version of a Chinese classic deserves a brief explanation.

Tsai Chih Chung (C.C. Tsai) is the most accomplished and popular cartoonist in all of East Asia, and portions of his books have been incorporated into the public school curriculum in Japan. C.C. began his career at the age of sixteen by publishing the first of what would be approximately two hundred "action" comic books. Following that, he went into the field of animation and garnered himself the Chinese equivalent of our Oscar, while building up the largest animation company in Taiwan. In his spare time, he turned to the humor of comic strips and put out the first daily comic strip in Taiwan newspapers.

One day on a flight to Japan, he began to sketch scenes from a book he was reading. The book had been written over two thousand years ago by a famous Daoist (Taoist) thinker named Zhuangzi (Chuang Tzu). From this emerged a new genre in the book world—a serious (though lighthearted) comic book explicating a profound topic. His aim was not to simplify, but to clarify. The ancient language in China is difficult for modern people to understand, so in addition to illustrating the subject matter, he also rendered the text into Modern Chinese.

When *Zhuangzi Speaks* came out in Taiwan, it shot to the top of the bestseller list, and the head of a major publishing company immediately remarked that it had world potential. Tired of all of his efforts on the daily strips and his new series on ancient Chinese thought, both of which were bringing him unparalleled fame for a cartoonist. Soon he held the four highest spots atop the bestseller list, until other authors insisted that comic books no longer be included on the list of "serious" literature. There are now over twenty books in C.C.'s series and millions of copies in print, and, just as predicted, they are rapidly gaining popularity all over the world.

Sunzi Speaks is the third of C.C. Tsai's books to be published in America and should appeal not only to readers of his previous American titles, *Zhuangzi Speaks* and *Zen Speaks,* but also to military purists and those trying to gain a competitive edge in any aspect of life. *The Art of War* by Sunzi is an ancient Chinese military classic, and *Sunzi Speaks* is a straightforward rendering of that text, with no special emphasis on nonmilitary interpretations, although the strategies delineated in the book have been successfully adopted by business leaders, politicians, and people from all walks of life interested in better negotiating human affairs.

Although C.C. Tsai provides a vernacular translation of the text in his Chinese version, for the English edition I have worked largely from the original Classical Chinese text, while referring to C.C.'s work as well as various English and Chinese interpretations. In addition, I have familiarized myself with the theories of some of the great military thinkers of the West, such as Napoleon, Clausewitz, Jomini, Moltke, and Fuller, in order to express Sunzi's ideas in the most appropriate terminology. I have not substituted business of other euphemisms for military terms, nor have I attempted to alter the original's already lucid style.

Clearly, *Sunzi Speaks* is a book of military principles—so how can it be extrapolated into other fields? The answer to this is that the book deals first and foremost with realism, with appraising circumstances and reacting intelligently and appropriately to them in order to tip the balance in one's favor.

Sunzi Speaks is a close adaptation of the Warring States Period (475-221B.C.) military classic *Sunzi Bingfa (Sun-tzu Ping-fa)*. Although commonly translated *The Art of War,* it would be more accurately rendered *The Principles and Tactics of Warfare.* In the context of this work, the word *bing* refers more to the general concept of warfare and all of its concomitant affairs than merely to operations on the battlefield. As for *fa,* although the romantic rendering of "art" is conceivably correct, and certainly appealing as a title, it is accurate only in the broadest sense. The word *fa* has the two fundamental meanings of "rule" and "method," so by extension, and as is perfectly evident from the content of the book, an ideal rendering of *fa* here would be "principles and tactics."

The panels at the margin of each page appeared in the Chinese version as supplementary material. We retain them here not because the information is essential but primarily because they add a nice decorative touch to the book.

I would like to thank Lian Xinda for his vetting of the manuscript, Elizabeth Wales for her administrative contributions, Roger Scholl for his untiring efforts as editor, and Robin Yates for writing a wonderful introduction on short notice.

—B.B.

Introduction

This little book, brilliantly adapted and illustrated by the modern Taiwanese artist Tsai Chih Chung, was composed more than two thousand years ago in ancient China and yet is considered by military experts the world over to contain the most profound reflections on the art of war ever conceived anywhere at any time. For centuries in China, it was the basis for all subsequent theorizing about the relations between war and peace, and the role of the military in society, and from the eleventh century A.D. was the first of the seven core texts required in the military examination system. In Japan, in late traditional times, it was studied assiduously by the mighty samurai, as it was in Vietnam, and in the early twentieth century Soviet advisers were amazed to find their Communist colleagues, including Mao Zedong and the extraordinary marshall Zhu De, analyzing its precepts and putting them into practice.[1] Today, in East Asia, Europe, and North America, executives are finding much benefit from studying it as they ponder business strategy in increasingly competitive and globalized markets.

How could this be? How could the principles enunciated by Sunzi so long ago in such a completely different cultural environment be of value and relevance to the late twentieth century? A casual glance at any one of the stories that follow will reveal this secret. But seeing is one thing; really understanding and applying the knowledge Sunzi reveals is quite another.

Who was Sunzi and what was the place of warfare in ancient China? What were his principles and what can we learn from his book? Mythologically speaking, the Chinese believed that warfare was initiated almost at the beginning of time when Chi You, a savage denizen later worshipped as the god of war, invented five kinds of weapons to revolt against his lord, the Yellow Emperor. The latter, after receiving instruction from the Dark Maiden, a goddess versed in the secret arts, was able, with the help of benevolent natural forces such as the wind, to defeat the rebel (see p. 102) and restore order and civilization in the world. In the Chinese Bronze Age (roughly 2000 to 400 B.C., the Xia, Shang, and Zhou dynasties, see p. 137), warfare was one of the two primary means by which the aristocratic elites were able to maintain control over their subject populations; the other was sacrifice to the ancestors. Sacrifice and war were the two activities said to be essential for the survival of the state. Sacrifice provided food for the ancestors and spirits and kept them well disposed toward the living. Warfare provided the means for that food: not only were captives sacrificed at the altars of the state, but the other spoils of war, too, were dedicated to the honor of the ancestors. Thus warfare was seen as part of the ritual structure that held the world of men and the world of the spirits together as one indissoluble whole.

In warfare, the aristocratic elite, riding on elaborately decorated chariots, jousted with each other according to codes of chivalry that resembled in many respects the codes of honor that we are familiar with from stories about the knights of medieval Europe. So, for example, two armies would agree upon the place and time for a battle, often decided by recourse to divination, and one would not attack until the other was completely ready for combat. Thus, by acting according to the precise details of the ritual code, they were able to show that they understood the moral basis of the human and cosmological order.

But Sunzi, whose given name was Wu ("the Martial") and who was born in the powerful state of Qi (modern Shandong province in eastern China), lived at a time known as the Spring and Autumn period, when the aristocratic elite was rapidly disappearing in the frequent and increasingly bloody wars waged between rival states. These states no longer recognized the authority of the Zhou dynasty to bring order to China; each was trying to gain as much territory at the expense of their neighbors as possible. Any means to advance their own interests were acceptable, as were any means to bring about the collapse of their rivals. Sunzi, a contemporary of the great philosopher Confucius (551–479 B.C.), for-

mulated the principles by which this new type of warfare was waged. He is said to have written a work in thirteen sections and to have presented this to the King of Wu (a different Wu from Sunzi's name), Helü, who reigned in the period 514 to 496 B.C. over an area in the lower Yangtze Valley and who was locked in a deadly combat with the neighboring state of Yue. This rivalry is frequently alluded to in *Sunzi* (for example, p. 123), and Tsai Chih Chung illustrates the king, wearing a rectangular crown with beads hanging down in front and rear. Helü's rivals are similarly drawn.

Little is actually known about Sunzi's life: the main incident is the story of him demonstrating his military expertise by drilling the brigade of King Helü's concubines (see pp. 14–20). This "biography" was even found in 1972 among a collection of texts that were buried in a Han dynasty tomb at Silver Sparrows Mountain around 140 B.C. These texts contain the earliest version of the *Sunzi* and include sections above and beyond the thirteen that Tsai presents here, sections that were lost in antiquity.[2] In the story, the main point that Sunzi is trying to convince the king of is that organization and discipline are the two most crucial aspects to winning in warfare. Insubordination must be punished no matter who commits it—in this case the king's two favorite ladies. Further, as warfare is of crucial importance to the survival of the state (see p. 23), once the ruler offers the command to a general and the latter accepts, it is only the general who issues orders: the ruler cannot countermand them (see p. 113). Rewards and punishments must be clear and carried out with strictness, fairness, and equanimity, and the general must possess exceptional knowledge and understanding of the principles of war and act only for the benefit of his country. The role of the ruler is to choose the very best general he can find and then let him get on with protecting his state and defeating his enemies. Delegation of authority to a single general is essential for victory: it is useless and even dangerous for the king to meddle in affairs he does not understand.

Sunzi generally rejects appeals to the supernatural that were becoming popular among rival groups of philosophers, such as the specialists in the transformations of yin and yang and the Five Elements or Phases, although he does occasionally allude to them,[3] and he consciously repudiates the type of war based on ritual performance that existed prior to his time. For him, warfare was an art of deception (see p. 32), and the only thing that mattered was winning: "In war, you must win; in attacking, you must take the initiative. If it is not beneficial to the country, do not take action. If you cannot win, do not go to war" (p. 128). Alas, this is wise advice that is all too frequently ignored by overambitious politicians and haughty generals anxious to make a name for themselves. Warfare for Sunzi, and most later Chinese, was a most unfortunate and inauspicious activity, but essential for survival; one must not glory in military adventure and heroism, but, lamenting its necessity, one should take all precautions to ensure success. Hence the importance Sunzi gave to spies (see pp. 130–37), for correct use of them allowed for the possibility that one could win without ever having to fight and kill.

As the reader will quickly become aware, Sunzi enjoyed classifying military factors into numbered sets, and this propensity suggests that his mode of argumentation was moving in the direction of what we might call scientific thinking. Most particularly, we can deduce approximately ten basic principles that formed the key concepts in the Chinese theory of war. It is these principles that are of perennial interest and value.[4] They are:

1. Act in accordance with a plan only after full consideration of the consequences.
2. Always seek maximum profit, preferably by not having to actually use force, for force is much more effective when it is only threatened.
3. Try not to damage your enemy, but rather capture him whole, for thereby your own profit will be increased.
4. Weaken the enemy before engaging him, for his resistance can be thereby diminished before the engagement and you are in consequence strengthened.
5. Force the enemy to do things he does not wish or expect to do, especially by manipulating the situation or circumstances to your own advantage.
6. Use the enemy's and one's own potential, intentions, and psychological

inclinations to one's own advantage, so that one can sweep the enemy away by the force of circumstances or the situation.

7. Strike always with your own fullest strength against the enemy's weakest points.

8. Always realize that there are advantages and disadvantages to every course of action. Make a full evaluation of these and turn your own disadvantages into advantages and the enemy's advantages into disadvantages.

9. Act always according to the changes in the natural course of things. Nothing stays the same and you must never, therefore, stick to a single course of action. Be aware of how the situation is altering and transform your own behavior to conform to the new circumstances.

10. Always seek to achieve your aims by indirect means that your enemy does not expect.

These principles are, of course, absolutely appropriate to every situation in life, but few indeed are able to put them into practice. It remains for you to see how Tsai Chih Chung illustrates Sunzi's precepts.

–Robin D. S. Yates
Director, Centre for East Asian Research
McGill University
Montreal, Canada

Notes:

1. Joseph Needham and Robin D. S. Yates et al., *Science and Civilisation in China*, Volume 5, Part 6, "Military Technology." Cambridge: Cambridge University Press, 1994.

2. For a translation of these texts, see Roger Ames, *Sun-Tzu: The Art of Warfare, the First English Translation Incorporating the Recently Discovered Yin-ch'üeh-shan Texts*. New York: Ballantine Books, 1993.

3. For example, see pp. 80, 126, and 132. The Five Phases Wood, Fire, Earth, Metal, and Water were natural principles that succeeded each other in turn through the cycle of the year and were correlated with other sets of five, including the seasons, spring, summer, late summer, fall, winter; the colors, green, red, yellow, white, black; the directions, east, south, center, west, and north; the numbers; and so on. It was believed that it was essential for humans to coordinate their activities to these natural, cosmological phases, for if one did not, all sorts of unpleasant results would occur, for example frost and snow would fall in summer, or there would be thunderstorms in the depths of winter when it should be cold. Later philosophers thought that each dynasty ruled in turn under the aegis of these phases, and so they adopted the colors, numbers, directions, and so forth in accordance with the system.

4. For a full discussion of them, see Needham and Yates, pp. 31–37.

SUNZI SPEAKS

THE ART OF WAR

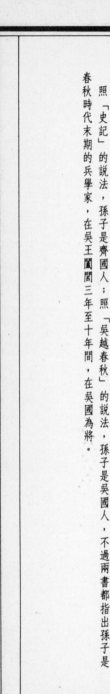

照「史記」的說法，孫子是齊國人；照「吳越春秋」的說法，孫子是吳國人，不過兩書都指出孫子是春秋時代末期的兵學家，在吳王闔閭三年至十年間，在吳國為將。

THE LIFE OF SUN WU

IT IS SAID THAT ABOUT 500 B.C., DURING THE SPRING & AUTUMN PERIOD IN CHINA, THERE LIVED A MAN WITH THE SURNAME SUN AND THE GIVEN NAME WU. OUT OF RESPECT FOR HIS GREATNESS, THE SUFFIX ZI IS ADDED TO HIS SURNAME, JUST LIKE KONGZI (CONFUCIUS), MENGZI (MENCIUS), AND ZHUANGZI. HE IS SAID TO HAVE LIVED IN THE STATE OF QI AND IS CREDITED WITH HAVING WRITTEN THE THIRTEEN CHAPTERS OF SUNZI BINGFA, OR SUNZI'S PRINCIPLES AND TACTICS OF WARFARE.

The ART of WAR

HE ONCE PRESENTED THIS BOOK TO KING HELÜ OF WU.

FANTASTIC! THIS IS WONDERFUL!

The ART of WAR

I HAVE READ YOUR BOOK, SIR, AND I AM WONDERING IF YOU COULD USE IT TO TRAIN A CONTINGENT HERE AND NOW.

OF COURSE I CAN.

COULD YOU DO IT USING WOMEN?

YES.

SO THE KING ORDERED ONE HUNDRED EIGHTY PALACE WOMEN INTO THE ARENA.

SUNZI THEN ORGANIZED THEM INTO TWO UNITS, WITH THE KING'S TWO FAVORITE CONCUBINES AS LEADERS.

THEN HE EQUIPPED EACH PERSON WITH THE WEAPON OF THE TIMES, THE DAGGER-AXE.

DO YOU ALL KNOW THE POSITIONS OF YOUR HEART, LEFT AND RIGHT HANDS, AND YOUR BACK?

YES.

YES.

在「史記」和「吳越春秋」都有孫子操練宮女的記載，不過後世多有所懷疑，宋代的葉適反對最力，他在「習學記言」上特別指出這是「誇大其詞，不足採信」。

15

16

司馬遷的「史記」和趙曄的「吳越春秋」是記載孫子事蹟較為詳細的兩部書，除此之外，荀子「議兵」篇、韓非子「五蠹」篇、國語「魏語」，都曾提到孫子善用兵，其他有關家世、出身等，則均無記載。

吳、楚原為世仇，吳子胥本來亦在楚國為官，因避禍而逃至吳，所以伐楚成為闔閭和吳子胥的共同目標，而孫子在受到賞識重用後，成為伐楚的大將。

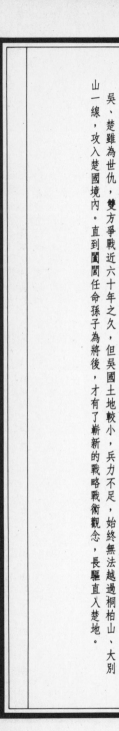

FORWARD MARCH.

ONE, TWO **ONE, TWO** **ONE, TWO**

DA-DUM!

SUNZI ORDERED TWO OTHER WOMEN TO BE UNIT LEADERS, AND THIS TIME, WHEN THE DRUM WAS STRUCK AND THE ORDERS WERE GIVEN, THEY OBEYED THE ORDERS COMPLETELY, AND NO ONE DARED LET OUT ANOTHER HEE-HEE OR HA-HA.

THE COMPANY HAS COMPLETED ITS EXERCISES IN AN ORDERLY FASHION. THE KING MAY DESCEND AND INSPECT HIS TROOPS.

THESE SOLDIERS WILL NOW OBEY ANY ORDER THE KING MAY GIVE, EVEN IF IT IS TO CROSS THROUGH BOILING WATER OR WALK ON FIRE.

WHY DON'T YOU PLEASE DISMISS THE TROOPS AND RETURN TO YOUR QUARTERS TO REST! I'M NOT IN THE MOOD TO GO DOWN AND WATCH.

THE KING LIKES MILITARY THEORY, BUT NOT THE APPLICATION OF IT ...

ALTHOUGH KING HELÜ WASN'T HAPPY ABOUT WHAT HAD JUST OCCURRED, HE UNDERSTOOD THAT SUNZI REALLY KNEW HOW TO ORGANIZE AN ARMY, AND LATER HE ENDED UP EMPLOYING SUNZI AS HIS GENERAL.

THEREAFTER HE TOOK HIS TINY COUNTRY OF WU AND THRUST WESTWARD INTO CHU, TAKING YING, THE CAPITAL, THEN HE WENT NORTH INTO THE CENTRAL PLAINS AND AWED THE STATES OF QI AND JIN.

SO THE REPUTATION OF WU SPREAD THROUGH ALL THE STATES OF THE SPRING & AUTUMN PERIOD, AND THE MAN BEHIND THE SCENES WAS NONE OTHER THAN SUNZI!

THE ART OF WAR

ATTACK LIKE FIRE

STILL LIKE A FOREST

IMMOVABLE LIKE A MOUNTAIN

FLEET LIKE THE WIND

SUNZI'S ARMY

吳王闔閭九年、周敬王十四年，西元前五○六年，吳軍終於攻破楚國國都郢，以一小國的少數兵力而能轉戰千里，大敗楚國這樣的一流強國，若非一代兵學大師孫子策畫，吳軍絕不可能有如此優異的表現，所以司馬遷在「史記」上稱讚說：「西破強楚，入郢，北威齊晉，顯名諸侯，孫子與有力焉。」

「始計」是孫子兵法十三篇之首，原來古本兵法沒有「始」字，只稱「計篇」，後來做註解的人才加上「始」字。

「計」的意思很廣泛，在這裡至少有三個含義：一是計畫、計謀；二是計算、比較；三是預計、分析。其目的就是說明戰爭前的各項準備工作，特別強調戰爭之勝負取決於戰前的籌畫。

CHAPTER 1

CALCULATION

由於戰爭之勝負關係國家之存亡，人民之生死，所以各種比較分析，務必非常慎重、籌畫精密，則取勝的公算大；籌畫草率，則取勝公算小，如果冒冒失失，毫無計畫的興兵作戰，則必難逃失敗的命運。

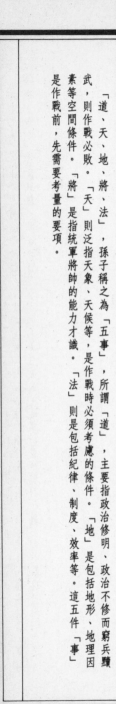

「道、天、地、將、法」，孫子稱之為「五事」，所謂「道」，主要指政治修明、政治不修而窮兵黷武，則作戰必敗。「天」則泛指天象、天候等，是作戰時必須考慮的條件。「地」是包括地形、地理因素等空間條件。「將」是指統軍將帥的能力才識。「法」則是包括紀律、制度、效率等。這五件「事」是作戰前，先需要考量的要項。

THE DAO, HEAVEN, EARTH, COMMAND, LAW

WE MUST LOOK AT WARFARE FROM FIVE DIFFERENT POINTS OF VIEW, COMPARING, CALCULATING, AND SEEKING THE FACTS.

THE FIRST IS REGULATING THE DAO, OR ESTABLISHING A MORAL CAUSE.

THE SECOND IS HEAVEN, OR CLIMATE.

THE THIRD IS THE EARTH, OR TERRAIN AND GEOGRAPHY.

THE FOURTH IS COMMAND, OR LEADERSHIP.

THE FIFTH IS THE LAW, OR DISCIPLINE.

24

孫子解釋「道」：「令民與上同意，可與之生；可與之死，而不畏危也。」這裡所應注意的是「令民與上同意」，所謂「同意」，就是人民與政府之間，有共同的信念、目標，要做到這樣，必須愛民、親民，唯有全民竭誠擁護的政府，才能使民眾無懼戰爭的危險，為實現共同的目標而奮戰。

春秋時代多迷信，「左傳」中記載兵戎之事也有許多卜問吉凶的例子，不過孫子並不是迷信的人，他所説的：「天者，陰陽、寒暑、時制也。」主要是指天候氣象之變化，沒有任何迷信的色彩。

26

所謂「地」，係指安營決戰之地，亦即主帥對有利的地理形勢和空間條件之利用特別重視。孫子在「九變」、「行軍」、「地形」、「九地」各篇中，反覆說明地形地物之利用要領，足見孫子對於「地利」之取得與否、做為衡量戰爭勝負的要件，其重視的程度，可以想見。

27

孫子認為「智、信、仁、勇、嚴」五者，是為將之道，不過要五者兼備，並不是容易的事，明朝何守法在註解這一段話說：「蓋專任智則賊；固守信則愚；惟施仁則懦；純恃勇則暴；一予嚴則殘。」這裡說的「賊、愚、懦、暴、殘」，正好是「智、信、仁、勇、嚴」的反面，為將帥者如行事偏頗，輕則身敗名裂，重則喪師辱國，不可不慎。

COMMAND

"COMMAND" REFERS TO THE CHARACTERISTICS THAT A LEADER OF TROOPS MUST POSSESS:

WISDOM, TRUSTWORTHINESS, BENEVOLENCE, COURAGE,

AND STERNNESS.

28

所謂「法」，就是制度化，軍事行動講求的是效率，要快速靈活，才能收如臂使指之效，這必須在平時就建立良好制度，戰時方能發揮力量，所以編制合理、人事上軌道、紀律賞罰嚴謹、財務軍需補給健全，便是克敵致勝的保障。

「七計」的工作是將帥在戰爭前所做的幕僚參謀工作，在各種比較分析中，得出結論，向國君提出建議，所以孫子說：「……吾以此知勝負矣，將聽吾計，用之必勝，留之；將不聽吾計，用之必敗，去之。」

「將」聽吾計：「將」讀做″⸺″，做語助詞，是「如果」的意思，「將」不聽吾計之「將」，其意亦同。另一種說法是「將」仍是指「將帥」而言，解釋亦可通。

孫子列舉的「詭道」計十二項：「能而示之不能」；「用而示之不用」；「近而示之遠」；「遠而示之近」；「利而誘之」；「亂而取之」；「實而備之」；「強而避之」；「怒而撓之」；「卑而驕之」；「佚而勞之」；「親而離之」，都是欺敵、乘敵的方法。

SUBTERFUGE

WARFARE IS DECEPTION— THE USE OF CLEVER TACTICS AND MOVEMENTS THAT ARE ALWAYS CHANGING.

WHEN YOU ARE CAPABLE OF FIGHTING, MAKE IT APPEAR THAT YOU ARE NOT.

HA-HA, LOOK HOW SMALL THEIR CAMP IS.

WHEN YOU WISH TO DO BATTLE, MAKE IT APPEAR THAT YOU DO NOT.

CEASE FIRE, TALK PEACE

WHEN ATTACKING NEARBY, MAKE IT APPEAR THAT YOU ARE ATTACKING AT A DISTANT POINT.

WHEN ATTACKING AT A DISTANT POINT, MAKE IT APPEAR THAT YOU ARE ATTACKING NEARBY.

LURE THE ENEMY WITH A SMALL ADVANTAGE;
SOW DISORDER AMONG THE RANKS OF THE ENEMY, AND ATTACK WHEN CHAOS ERUPTS;
WHEN THE ENEMY EXHIBITS NO WEAK POINTS, FULLY READY YOUR OWN SIDE;
WHEN THE ENEMY IS STRONG, AVOID HIM;
TAUNT THE ENEMY INTO ANGER;
FEIGN WEAKNESS TO CREATE OVERCONFIDENCE IN THE ENEMY;
WHEN THE ENEMY NEEDS REST, KEEP HIM ACTIVE;
WHEN THE ENEMY IS UNIFIED, SEEK TO SPLINTER HIM.

TAKING ADVANTAGE OF THE ENEMY

The ART of WAR

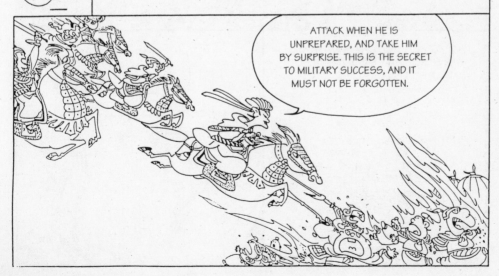

ATTACK WHEN HE IS UNPREPARED, AND TAKE HIM BY SURPRISE. THIS IS THE SECRET TO MILITARY SUCCESS, AND IT MUST NOT BE FORGOTTEN.

孫子雖然說：「兵者，詭道也。」但詭詐計謀並非致勝之唯一要素，為將帥者更不可一味好用詐術，所以孫子先強調「道、天、地、將、法」五事，然後才談詭道，「五事」是恒久不變的原則，「詭道」只是針對一時一地特殊情況應變的手段，這只要看孫子說：「計利以聽，乃為之勢，以佐其外。」便可知其主從、本末了，作戰斷不能不用「詭道」，但亦不能全依「詭道」，這是孫子強調的原則。

33

「廟」是指宗廟、祖廟而言，古代出師，必先集於廟堂之上，告祭祖先、以示鄭重，同時亦乘此機會集合討論。所以「廟算」等於今日之最高決策會議，以決定要不要戰？能不能戰？如何作戰？

TEMPLE DECISIONS

BEFORE A WAR HAS BEGUN, FIRST GO TO THE TEMPLE AND DETERMINE THE STRONG AND WEAK POINTS OF EACH SIDE.

IF WE HAVE MORE ADVANTAGES, OUR CHANCES OF WINNING ARE GREATER.

IF WE HAVE FEWER ADVANTAGES, OUR CHANCES OF WINNING ARE SMALLER.

WITH CORRECT CALCULATIONS, A WAR CAN BE WON. YOU CANNOT WIN WITH INCORRECT CALCULATIONS, LET ALONE NO CALCULATIONS AT ALL.

IF EXAMINED WITH THIS IN MIND, VICTORY AND DEFEAT CAN BE PREDICTED.

CHAPTER 2

WAGING WAR

「作戰」篇主要在說明戰爭對國家和人民所產生的沉重負擔，任何一個國家都無法經得起長時期的戰爭損耗、所以作戰愈快取得勝利，愈能減少自身損失而獲取戰果，因此孫子特別強調：「兵貴速，不貴久。」

A MILLION DOLLARS A DAY

SUNZI SAID: AS FOR THE PRINCIPLES AND TACTICS OF WARFARE, IN PREPARING FOR WAR, YOU WILL NEED ONE THOUSAND CHARIOTS AND ONE THOUSAND SUPPLY WAGONS.

THESE WILL ACCOMPANY ONE HUNDRED THOUSAND ARMORED SOLDIERS, AND FOOD WILL HAVE TO BE TRANSPORTED ONE THOUSAND MILES ...

ADD ON THE EXPENDITURES FOR DIPLOMACY, INTELLIGENCE RE-PORTS, SUPPLEMENTAL PROVISIONS, AND MAINTENANCE OF EQUIPMENT, AND THE TOTAL WILL BE A GREAT SUM OF MONEY EVERY DAY;

AND ONLY WHEN ALL THESE ARE PREPARED CAN A CONTINGENT OF ONE HUNDRED THOUSAND SOLDIERS SET OUT.

按周代井田制度，八家為井；四井為邑；四邑為丘；四丘為甸，作戰時，每甸出戎馬四匹；牛十六頭；駟車一乘；重車一輛；甲士步卒一百人；正好符合前述的戰鬥編組。不過以此推算，每「甸」計五百十二戶人家，需出丁壯一百人，就動員數量來說，相當驚人。不過到春秋末期，井田制度已非原來面貌，軍旅動員亦不可能全按這種比例，但無論如何，興師十萬的場面，仍需非常龐大的後勤支援力量的。

戰爭既然要耗費龐大的人力、物力、財力，所以大軍出征作戰，以爭取勝利為首要，時間拖得愈久，則愈使軍隊疲憊，銳氣盡失，同時長久征戰，亦必使國家財政枯竭，所以孫子強調：「兵貴勝，不貴久

。」

VICTORY, NOT DURATION

WINNER LOSER

IN WAR, YOU SHOULD FIGHT AND RESOLVE IT QUICKLY. DON'T DRAG IT OUT BY SHOWING OFF YOUR MILITARY MIGHT.

WHEN WAR IS PROTRACTED, THERE IS ABSOLUTLEY NO BENEFIT TO THE COUNTRY.

THE LONGER THE WAR, THE MORE AND GREATER DAMAGE DONE, AND EVEN IF YOU WIN, THE GAINS WILL NOT MAKE UP FOR THE LOSSES. AIM FOR VICTORY, NOT DURATION. BY QUICKLY DEFEATING THE ENEMY AND RESOLVING THE CONFLICT, YOU WILL AVOID TIRING AND ANGERING THE PEOPLE AND MIRING YOUR COUNTRY IN WAR, WHICH WOULD SURELY LEAD TO A COLLAPSE OF THE ECONOMY.

GAIN STRENGTH THROUGH DEFEATING THE ENEMY

IF YOU DO NOT UNDERSTAND THE HARM THAT MILITARY ACTIONS CAUSE, THEN YOU CANNOT UNDERSTAND THE BENEFITS TO BE GAINED THROUGH MILITARY ACTION.

BENEFIT

HARM

CONSCRIPTION NOTICE

AFTER ONE DRAFT, AN ABLE MILITARY COMMANDER WILL NEVER IMPLEMENT A SECOND LEVY,

DRAFT

ORDERS

IF WE DON'T HAVE ENOUGH GRAIN IN OUR OWN COUNTRY, WE'LL GET IT FROM THE ENEMY.

HE WILL ALSO NEVER CREATE THE NEED TO SHIP GRAIN MORE THAN TWICE.

WHAT IF WE RUN OUT?

孫子説：「役不再籍，糧不三載。」就是僅做一次動員召集，迅速擊敗敵人，迅速結束戰爭，不要再做第二次的動員，以免招致民怨。至於糧食之裝載輸送，也僅兩次為限絕不超過三次，以免國內糧食不足，發生缺糧現象。

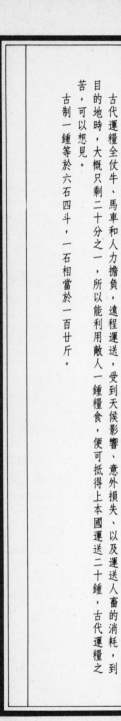

孫子強調「因糧於敵」、「智將務食於敵」，就是「以戰養戰」的思想，同時為了鼓勵士卒，必須「賞其先得者」，讓士卒能爭先掠取敵人的物資，以做為自己的戰利品，壯大自己的力量。

THE GENERAL WHO KNOWS

QUICK TO FIGHT, QUICK TO END IT!

MILITARY ACTIONS SHOULD TAKE VICTORY AS THEIR MAIN OBJECTIVE AND SHOULD NEVER BE ALLOWED TO GO ON TOO LONG.

A GENERAL WHO UNDERSTANDS HOW TO FIGHT A WAR KNOWS THAT HE HOLDS THE SURVIVAL OF THE PEOPLE IN HIS HANDS AND IS THE PROTECTOR OF THE COUNTRY'S PEACE.

AN ABLE MILITARY COMMANDER STRENGTHENS HIS FORCES, MAKES THE ENEMY'S STRENGTHS HIS OWN, HAS A PROFOUND UNDERSTANDING OF THE DANGERS OF PROTRACTED WAR, AND AIMS AT ENDING A MILITARY ACTION AS SOON AS POSSIBLE. THEREFORE, THE GENERAL WHO UNDERSTANDS WARFARE IS THE KEY TO PEACE IN A COUNTRY!

不過「以戰養戰」，並非絕對可行，如果敵人實行「堅壁清野」，則「因糧於敵」、「務食於敵」，必成空想，所以用兵必須要迅速機動，在敵人料想不到的時間、地點，乘虛而入，敵人來不及破壞一切，才能享受到勝利的戰果，因此孫子在本篇結尾時仍再三強調「兵貴勝，不貴久」。

CHAPTER 3
STRATEGIC OFFENSIVE

「謀攻」主要在說明沒有戰場的戰鬥行為，戰場上殺伐熾烈，不論勝負均會有所損失，因此最理想的方式是不經戰鬥而取得勝利，想做到這點就必須運用謀略方法和外交手段，達到使敵人屈服的目的，這就是「不戰而屈人之兵」，是用兵的最高明境界。

THE PRINCIPLES AND TACTICS OF WARFARE

SUNZI SAID:

AS FOR THE PRINCIPLES AND TACTICS OF WARFARE, KEEPING THE COUNTRY WHOLE IS BETTER THAN BRINGING HARM TO IT, EVEN IF VICTORY WERE TO BE GAINED.

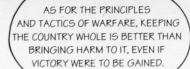

KEEPING THE ARMY WHOLE IS BETTER THAN BRINGING HARM TO IT. KEEPING A BATTALION WHOLE IS BETTER THAN BRINGING HARM TO IT. KEEPING A COMPANY WHOLE IS BETTER THAN BRINGING HARM TO IT. KEEPING A SQUAD WHOLE IS BETTER THAN BRINGING HARM TO IT.

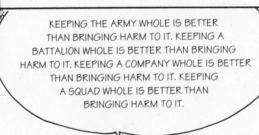

用兵的上策是既能取得勝利，又能保全自己實力，因此用謀略的方式；不經血戰而能屈服敵人軍旅，是最高境界，所以孫子在本篇一開始就提出五個「全」字——全國、全軍、全旅、全卒、全伍，就是強調以「全」爭天下，也就是希望在不傷絲毫的情況下，取得「全勝」。

THEREFORE, FIGHTING AND WINNING A HUNDRED WARS IS NOT THE GREATEST GOOD.

THE GREATEST GOOD IS GETTING THE ENEMY TO SURRENDER WITHOUT EVER HAVING TO FIGHT.

KILL!

HA-HA ... I WON WITHOUT FIGHTING!

孫子說：「百戰百勝，非善之善者也；不戰而屈人之兵，善之善者也。」要想不戰而勝，唯有使用政治、外交等手段，造成敵人不得不屈服我的形勢，才能達到兵不血刃的目的，這便是「伐謀」與「伐交」。

「伐謀」就是謀略戰，運用智謀，訂出適切的政略，誘使敵人處處被動，舉棋不定，驚惶失措，而使我方能以最小的代價，獲致最大的戰果。「伐交」則是外交戰，係利用外交策略，分化敵人之盟友，聯合我方之友邦，使敵人陷於孤立無援境地。戰爭最高境界，就是使敵人陷於進退兩難，不知所措，而我方則乘此良機，予取予求。

ATTACK STRATEGY

THE BEST PLAN IN WAR IS TO ATTACK THROUGH THE USE OF CUNNING STRATEGY.

1+1 = ?

USE YOUR BRAIN TO BEAT THE ENEMY!

?

!

THE NEXT BEST PLAN IS TO ATTACK THE ENEMY THROUGH ALLIANCES, FORCING THE ENEMY TO CAPITULATE.

AFTER THAT, THE BEST STRATEGY IS TO ATTACK THE ENEMY USING A STRONG ARMY, THEREBY FORCING HIM TO SURRENDER.

SURRENDER!

I SURRENDER!

THE WORST PLAN IS TO LAY SIEGE TO A FORTIFIED CITY!

SHOULD WE ATTACK?

I THINK AT THIS STAGE WE HAVE NO CHOICE....

LAYING SIEGE TO A CITY SHOULD ONLY BE DONE UNDER THE MOST DESPERATE OF CIRCUMSTANCES. BEGIN THE PRELIMINARIES TO LAYING SIEGE!

MANUFACTURING LARGE SHIELDS, SIEGE WEAPONS, AND ALL KINDS OF MACHINERY TAKES THREE MONTHS TO COMPLETE.

BUILDING EARTHEN RAMPARTS FOR MOUNTING WALLS TAKES ANOTHER THREE MONTHS TO COMPLETE....

孫子最反對的便是硬碰硬的「攻城」，古代攻奪城池，既耗人力、物力，又曠久費時，與「兵貴速，不貴久」的原則相背，攻城必經惡戰，惡戰必有重大傷亡，與「全勝」原則相反，當然是最不宜採取的方式。

古代攻城，傷亡率極高，所以孫子說：「殺士卒三分之一，而城不拔者，此攻之災也。」與「伐謀」、「伐交」、「伐兵」來比較，攻城當然是最下策，也是最難奏效的方式。

IF A GENERAL FEELS THAT THIS IS TOO SLOW AND, UNABLE TO CONTROL HIS FURY, HE ORDERS THE SOLDIERS TO ATTACK LIKE SO MANY ANTS, ONE THIRD OF THEM WILL DIE ...

AND THE WALL WILL REMAIN STANDING. THIS IS THE SAD CALAMINTY OF BESIEGING CITIES.

SO AN ABLE MILITARY COMMANDER CAN GET THE ENEMY TO SURRENDER WITHOUT FIGHTING;

I LOSE!

CAN CAPTURE THE ENEMY'S CITY WITHOUT LAYING SIEGE TO IT;

SURRENDER

AND HE CAN DESTROY THE ENEMY COUNTRY WITHOUT ENGAGING IN A PROTRACTED WAR.

「伐謀」與「伐交」都是沒有戰場的戰鬥，都是利用敵人的心理弱點及現實利害，步步進逼，處處主動，所謂不越樽俎之間，折衝千里之外，造成敵人不得不屈服的形勢，這就是孫子所強調的「不戰而屈之兵」。

「伐謀」與「伐交」很難區分其先後層次，不過善「伐謀」者必善於「伐交」；善「伐交」者亦善「伐謀」，兩者常交互為用。處處把握以「全爭天下」的原則，「兵不頓」（沒有重大傷亡）；「利可全」（戰果完整），就是「伐謀」、「伐交」的最高境界。

50

孫子認為我方如在優勢兵力情況下，可以「十則圍之，五則攻之，倍則分之。」如果在兵力相當或屬於劣勢時，可以「敵則能戰之，少則能守之，不若則能避之。」的方式，這是屬於野戰戰法的要領，是佔在「量」的觀念上談作戰方式，也就是依敵我兵力的多寡，來決定作戰方式。

IF YOUR NUMBERS ARE EQUAL WITH THE ENEMY'S ...

GAIN VICTORY THROUGH CLEVER TACTICS.

FIRST, FIND THE ENEMY'S WEAK POINTS, THEN ATTACK THEM.

COME OUT HERE AND FIGHT LIKE A REAL ARMY SO WE CAN FINISH THIS ONCE AND FOR ALL!

IF YOUR NUMBERS ARE SMALLER THAN THE ENEMY'S, TEMPORARILY MAINTAIN A PROTECTED POSITION SO AS TO AVOID A DECISIVE BATTLE.

IF YOU'RE SO TOUGH, COME IN HERE!

IF YOUR FORCES ARE FAR INFERIOR TO THE ENEMY'S, EVADE HIM.

GET BACK HERE AND FIGHT!

I HAVE TO USE MY HIT-AND-RUN GUERRILLA TACTICS. I CAN'T FIGHT YOU HEAD ON.

TO CONCLUDE, IF A SMALL ARMY STUBBORNLY TAKES ON A LARGE ARMY WITHOUT FIRST CONSIDERING ITS OWN SIZE ...

ALL RIGHT, LET'S GET IT OVER WITH RIGHT NOW!

IT WILL BE TAKEN PRISONER BY THE LARGER ARMY.

I GIVE UP!

WHEN YOUR FORCES ARE STRONGER THAN THE ENEMY'S, SURROUND HIM, ATTACK HIM, AND DIVIDE HIM. WHEN YOUR FORCES DON'T MEASURE UP TO THE ENEMY'S, BE ABLE TO FIGHT, BE ABLE TO HOLD YOUR GROUND, AND BE ABLE TO EVADE HIM. IN ADDITION, THERE MUST BE EXCEPTIONAL LEADERSHIP TO ATTAIN THE GOALS OF FIGHTING, HOLDING GROUND, AND EVADING THE ENEMY, OTHERWISE THERE WILL BE THE DANGER OF SUFFERING AN AGONIZING DEFEAT.

孫子所舉的野戰要領，含有兩項基本概念：一是主動；二是彈性。孫子所說的「圍之」、「攻之」、「分之」、「戰之」、「守之」、「避之」，無一不是主動原則和彈性原則的運用，因此絕不能墨守成規，一陳不變，必須要把握戰機，彈性應變。

將帥統軍，負國家之重任，繫天下之安危，因此統帥權之完整，非常重要。而古代國君卻往往顧忌軍權旁落，又恐懼將帥功高震主，懷有二心，所以對統帥權的授予，常有戒懼，所以形成統帥權應否獨立的問題。

POWERS OF THE COMMANDER

THE GENERAL IS THE PILLAR OF A COUNTRY.

IF THE GENERAL'S CHARACTER AND ABILITIES ARE WITHOUT REPROACH, THE COUNTRY WILL BE STRONG ...

IF THEY ARE LACKING, THE COUNTRY WILL BE WEAK.

THERE ARE THREE WAYS A SOVEREIGN CAN HARM THE ARMY ...

ONE: HE CAN ORDER THE ARMY TO ADVANCE WHEN THEY SHOULDN'T OR RETREAT WHEN THEY SHOULDN'T. THIS IS CALLED MEDDLING IN MILITARY OPERATIONS.

TWO: NOT UNDERSTANDING MILITARY AFFAIRS, HE CAN RECKLESSLY INTERFERE WITH MILITARY ADMINISTRATION, THUS CONFUSING THE OFFICERS AND MEN SO THAT THEY ARE NOT SURE WHAT TO DO.

THREE: NOT UNDERSTANDING THE STRATEGY AND VARIATIONS OF WARFARE, HE CAN TAKE ON THE DUTIES OF A GENERAL, THUS CAUSING DOUBT AMONG THE OFFICERS AND MEN.

ADVANCE

RETREAT

WHO ARE WE SUPPOSED TO LISTEN TO?

I DON'T KNOW EITHER....

孫子認為國君侵犯統帥權之後遺症有三：即「縻軍」、「惑軍」、「疑軍」，這三種禍患都是干涉軍旅的指揮系統，影響戰略戰術的執行，因此孫子堅決反對國君對統帥權有任何干預或牽制。

孫子說：「知勝者有五：知可以戰與不可以戰者勝；識眾寡之用者勝；上下同欲者勝；以虞待不虞者勝；將能而君不御者勝。」這五項比較條件，是統帥衡量形勢，決定戰略戰術的運用，與第一篇「始計」中的「廟算」，略有不同，「廟算」是決定國家「大戰略」，這裡所謂的「知勝」，則是將帥在軍事戰略或野戰戰略、戰術的考量。

IF CONFUSION OR DOUBT TAKES HOLD IN YOUR ARMY, THE ENEMY WILL TAKE ADVANTAGE AND ADVANCE. SO WE SAY, CAUSING HAVOC IN ONE'S OWN ARMY LEADS TO VICTORY FOR THE ENEMY.

THERE ARE FIVE POINTS THAT CAN HELP CALCULATE WHICH SIDE WILL BE VICTORIOUS:

1. THEY WHO KNOW WHEN TO FIGHT AND WHEN NOT TO FIGHT WILL WIN.
2. THEY WHO KNOW HOW MANY MEN TO DEPLOY WILL WIN.
3. THEY WHO CAN ESTABLISH A MORAL CAUSE BETWEEN THE GOVERNMENT AND THE PEOPLE WILL WIN.
4. THEY WHO ARE WELL PREPARED WHILE THE ENEMY IS ILL PREPARED WILL WIN.
5. THEY WHOSE GENERAL IS CAPABLE AND WHOSE SOVEREIGN DOES NOT INTERFERE WILL WIN.

THE OUTCOME OF A CONFLICT CAN BE PREDICTED ACCORDING TO THESE FIVE CRITERIA.

KNOW THYSELF, KNOW THINE ENEMY

I KNOW MY OWN STRONG POINTS,

AND I KNOW THE ENEMY'S WEAK POINTS.

BY UNDERSTANDING THE ENEMY AND YOURSELF, YOU CAN ENGAGE IN A HUNDRED BATTLES WITHOUT EVER BEING IN DANGER.

I DON'T UNDERSTAND THE ENEMY, BUT I UNDERSTAND MYSELF VERY WELL.

IF YOU UNDERSTAND YOURSELF WITHOUT UNDERSTANDING THE ENEMY, YOUR CHANCES OF WINNING ARE 50-50.

為將帥者，必須有「知彼知己」的能力，孫子特別強調「自知之明」，他認為「不知彼而知己」，一勝一負。」也就是勝負機會各半。如「不知彼」，又「不知己」，必然會「每戰必敗」，可見孫子對於「知己」的重視程度。

57

CHAPTER 4

TACTICAL DISPOSITION

善用兵者，在整體形勢上先做到不敗的地步，在戰爭準備與戰略佈置上求其萬全，這就是「先勝佈署」，孫子說：「先為不可勝，以待敵之可勝」，這種「不可勝」是操之在我，有賴於萬全的準備工作，但是戰勝敵人却不是勉強可以辦到的，所以孫子說：「勝可知，不可為。」就是這個意思。

THE OBJECTIVE OF STRATEGY

PRIOR TO WAR, THE GREAT GENERALS OF THE PAST WOULD STRENGTHEN THEIR OWN SIDE BOTH MORALLY AND MATERIALLY, AND THEN THEY WOULD WAIT FOR AN OPPORTUNITY TO ATTACK THE ENEMY.

WHETHER OR NOT MY ARMY CAN BE DEFEATED DEPENDS ON ME.

WHETHER OR NOT THE ENEMY MAKES A MISTAKE THAT WOULD ALLOW ME THE OPPORTUNITY TO GAIN VICTORY DEPENDS ON HIM.

SO WE SEE THAT THE GREAT GENERAL CAN PROTECT HIMSELF FROM GIVING THE ENEMY AN OPPORTUNITY FOR VICTORY, BUT HE CANNOT MAKE THE ENEMY SUSCEPTIBLE TO DEFEAT.

THEREFORE, IT IS SAID, VICTORY CAN BE KNOWN BUT NOT MADE. IN OTHER WORDS, VICTORY CAN BE PREDICTED, BUT WHETHER OR NOT THE ENEMY GIVES US AN OPPORTUNITY CANNOT BE FORCED.

DEFEND

WHEN WE CANNOT DEFEAT THE ENEMY, WE SHOULD TAKE UP A DEFENSIVE POSITION.

ATTACK

WHEN WE CAN DEFEAT THE ENEMY, WE SHOULD ENGAGE BATTLE.

孫子說：「不可勝者，守也；可勝者，攻也。」我不攻擊人，自無從取勝，人不攻擊我，亦無失敗之理，所以說「不可勝」。至於攻擊則是主動，集中兵力攻敵弱點，發揮壓倒性優勢，所以說是「可勝」。但無論攻、守，必先衡量自己的條件，本身條件不是即採守勢，有充分條件則採攻勢。

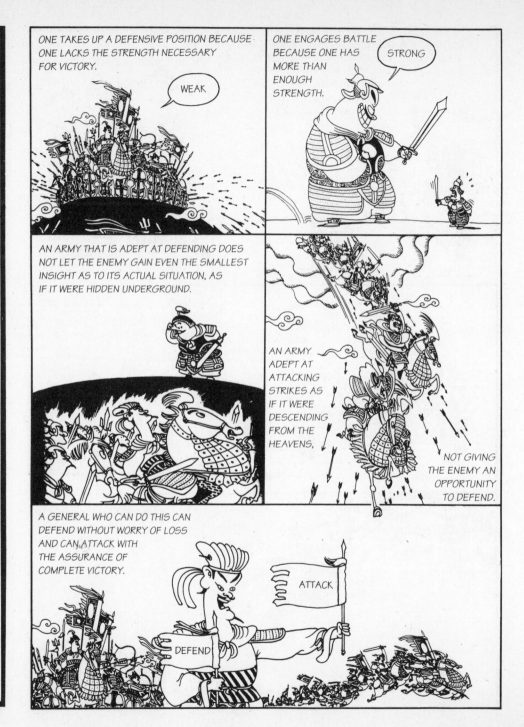

無論攻勢或守勢，都是換取所需要的時間，攻勢是在動態中換取所需時間；守勢是在靜態中換取所需時間，前者是在一定時間內，用積極的行動，捕捉敵人主力而消滅之，後者則是爭取時間，延緩敵人行動，伺機決戰。孫子形容「攻」與「守」說：「善守者，藏於九地之下；善攻者，動於九天之上。」

62

SEEK VICTORY BEFORE FIGHTING

THE ABLE MILITARY COMMANDER FIRST STANDS ON A FOUNDATION OF INVINCIBILITY, NOT GIVING THE ENEMY A SINGLE OPPORTUNITY TO TAKE ADVANTAGE OF,

AND HE DOESN'T MISS HIS CHANCE TO DEFEAT THE ENEMY.

SO WE SEE, THE VICTORIOUS PERSON CREATES THE CONDITIONS FOR CERTAIN VICTORY AND THEN DOES BATTLE WITH THE ENEMY.

NOW THAT WE ARE ASSURED VICTORY, STRIKE AND DEFEAT THE ENEMY.

KILL!

善用兵者，在整體形勢上先要做到不敗的要求，即或敵人知難而退。如果敵人在力量上超過我甚多，我也可以使其在「貨彈力屈」、「鈍兵挫銳」之餘，露出弱點，再逐次扭轉戰局、這就是「先勝求戰」之道。敵人傾國來犯，我已有充分準備，可以自保，使

AND WHAT OF THE DEFEATED PERSON?

WHAT ARE OUR CHANCES THIS TIME OUT?

FORGET THAT. FIGHT FIRST AND ASK QUESTIONS LATER!

HE ALWAYS ENGAGES THE ENEMY FIRST ...

THEN HOPES THAT HE IS LUCKY ENOUGH TO WIN.

OH NO! I NEVER THOUGHT THE ENEMY WOULD BE THIS STRONG!

AS FOR THE VICTORY OF AN ABLE MILITARY COMMANDER, HE DOES NOT REVEAL HIS STRATEGY, NOR CAN YOU SEE THE EFFORT BEHIND HIS VALOR. THIS IS BECAUSE HIS BATTLE IS BEGUN WITH THE CONFIDENCE OF SUCCESS, AND THE REASON FOR HIS CONFIDENCE IS THAT ALL OF HIS TACTICS STAND ON A FOUNDATION OF VICTORY. NATURALLY HE CAN OVERCOME THOSE ENEMIES THAT HAVE ALREADY REVEALED SIGNS OF DEFEAT.

The ART of WAR

THE CIRCUMSTANCES OF DECISIVE BATTLE

THE ABLE MILITARY COMMANDER BRINGS ENLIGHTENMENT TO THE MILITARY ADMINISTRATION AND UPHOLDS REGULATIONS. BECAUSE OF THIS, HE IS ABLE TO CONTROL VICTORY AND DEFEAT.

AS FOR THE PRINCIPLES AND TACTICS OF WARFARE, THERE ARE:

I: MEASUREMENT—JUDGING THE TERRAIN AND POSSIBLE BATTLE LINES.
II: APPRAISAL—ESTIMATING THE NECESSARY KINDS OF FORCE.
III: CALCULATION—CALCULATING THE AMOUNT OF TROOPS AND MATERIALS.
IV: DELIBERATION—WEIGHING THE ADVANTAGES AND DISADVANTAGES OF THE TWO SIDES.
V: VICTORY.

THE LAND DICTATES THE MEASUREMENT.

THE MEASUREMENT DICTATES THE APPRAISAL.

THE APPRAISAL DICTATES THE CALCULATION.

THE CALCULATION DICTATES THE DELIBERATION.

AND THE DELIBERATION DICTATES THE POSSIBILITY OF VICTORY.

孫子舉出「度」、「量」、「數」、「稱」、「勝」五個計算程序，以做為預測勝利的要訣。這是對「五事」、「七計」的補充，可以視之為軍事戰略佈署的要領。同時，孫子又再度談到「修道保法」，以政治修明、法制上軌道，為勝利之基礎，可見軍事與政治實有不可分的關係。

THE VICTOR CONCENTRATES ALL OF HIS TANGIBLE AND INTANGIBLE ADVANTAGES ON THE PLACE OF DECISIVE BATTLE AND IS LIKE THE WEIGHT OF A TON COMPARED TO THE WEIGHT OF A POUND. CONVERSELY, THE VANQUISHED IS AT A DISTINCT DISADVANTAGE.

THE VICTOR GIVING BATTLE IS LIKE OBSTRUCTED WATER SUDDENLY BURSTING OVER THE EDGE OF A THOUSAND-FOOT-HIGH CHASM. THESE ARE THE INVINCIBLE TACTICAL DISPOSITIONS.

CHAPTER 5

FORCE

「兵勢」主要在說明「勢」的運用，「勢」是力量的表現，如水勢、火勢，軍旅由靜止之狀態，迅速運動，所形成的威力，就是「兵勢」，這一篇與前面的「軍形」；後面的「虛實」，有承先啟後的連帶關係。

兵勢首要在作戰佈署，所以孫子在本篇起首即講「分數」、「形名」、「奇正」、「虛實」。

「分數」是部隊編組；「形名」是號令指揮；「奇正」是戰法變化；「虛實」是制敵弱點，這些都是兵勢部署之要點。

進一步說，「分數」、「形名」是指揮；「奇正」、「虛實」是戰術，正確的指揮配合高明的戰術，才能發揮兵旅的威勢。

孫子說：「凡戰者，以正合，以奇勝。」所謂「正」是常道，是不變的原則；所謂「奇」是權謀，是因時地人事而制宜的變化手段。拿「孫子兵法」為例，「五事」、「七計」是「正」；詭道權變是「奇」。伐謀為「正」、伐兵為「奇」。軍形為正；兵勢為「奇」。奇正相互配合，缺一不可。

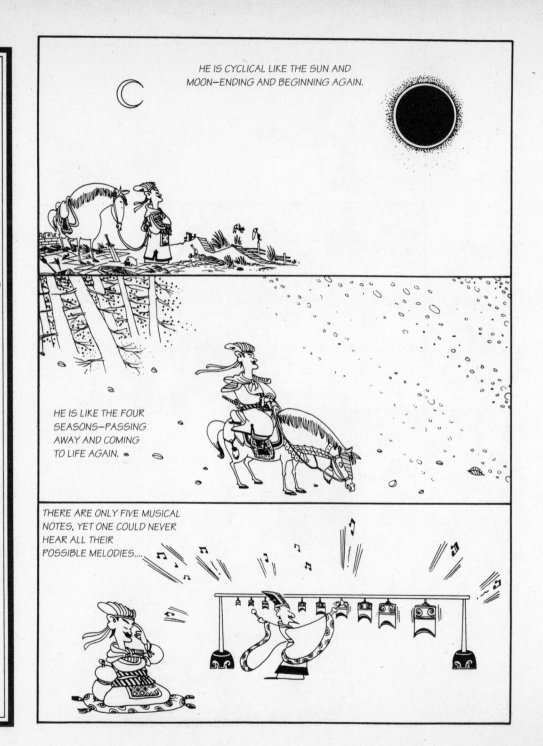

THERE ARE ONLY FIVE COLORS, YET ONE COULD NEVER SEE ALL OF THEIR POSSIBLE SHADES.

THERE ARE ONLY FIVE TASTES, YET ONE COULD NEVER TRY ALL OF THEIR POSSIBLE BLENDS.

FRONTAL AND SURPRISE CONFRONTATIONS ARE THE ONLY TWO KINDS OF FORCE FOR WAGING WAR, YET THEIR POSSIBLE COMBINATIONS ARE LIMITLESS. THEIR MUTUAL TRANSFORMATION IS LIKE TRACING THE LINE OF A CIRCLE—THERE IS NO ENDPOINT.

孫子說：「聲不過五，五聲之變，不可勝聽也。色不過五，五色之變，不可勝觀也。味不過五，五味之變，不可勝嘗也。戰勢不過奇正，奇正之變，不可勝窮也。」就是拿聲音、顏色、味覺的變化，證明戰勢中奇正之變，雖簡易實複雜多變。

71

戦場交鋒，不但是動作的比賽，而且是力量的較量，譬如猛鷲之撲擊，先斂其翼，這就是「形」，一旦動作完成，虛實強弱測定，飛掠而下，一撲中的，這就是「勢」的運用，所以將帥隨時要注意，把自己的力量發揮到極致，以克敵取勝。

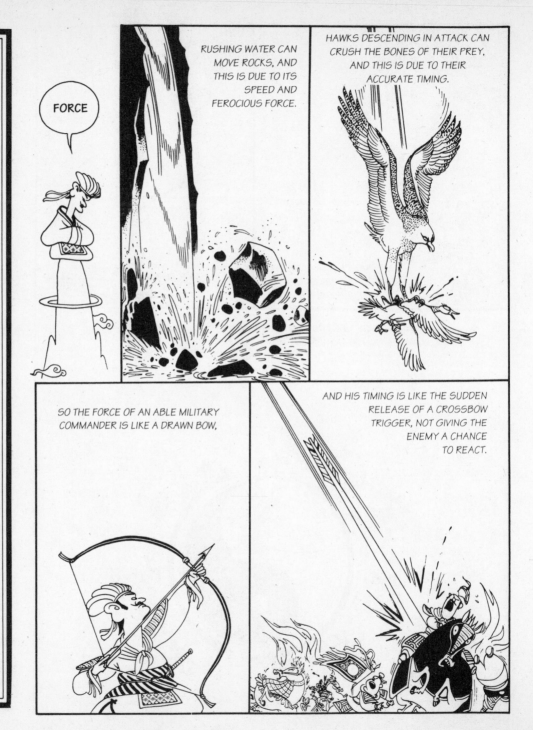

FORCE

RUSHING WATER CAN MOVE ROCKS, AND THIS IS DUE TO ITS SPEED AND FEROCIOUS FORCE.

HAWKS DESCENDING IN ATTACK CAN CRUSH THE BONES OF THEIR PREY, AND THIS IS DUE TO THEIR ACCURATE TIMING.

SO THE FORCE OF AN ABLE MILITARY COMMANDER IS LIKE A DRAWN BOW,

AND HIS TIMING IS LIKE THE SUDDEN RELEASE OF A CROSSBOW TRIGGER, NOT GIVING THE ENEMY A CHANCE TO REACT.

72

CREATING FORCE

AN ABLE MILITARY COMMANDER SEEKS VICTORY THROUGH FORCE BUT DOES NOT DEMAND IT FROM HIS MEN ALONE.

BECAUSE OF THIS, HE CAN CHOOSE MEN AND UTILIZE FORCE.

ONE WHO UTILIZES FORCE EMPLOYS HIS MEN AS IF ROLLING LOGS OR STONES DOWN A HILL. IT IS THE NATURE OF LOGS AND STONES THAT ON LEVEL GROUND THEY REMAIN STILL,

AND ON A SLOPE, THEY MOVE.

孫子用許多比喻來說明「造勢」，如：「激水之疾，至於漂石者，勢也。」「勢如張弩，節如機發。」等，都是在說明「造勢」是將帥之責，「善戰者，求之於勢，不責於人，故能擇人任勢。」「轉圓石於千仞之山者，勢也。」

73

SO THE FORCE THAT A COMMANDER CREATES IS LIKE A ROUND LOG OR ROCK PLUNGING DOWNWARD FROM A THOUSAND FEET UP,

AND ITS FEROCITY IS UNSTOPPABLE. THIS IS WHAT IS MEANT BY FORCE.

「形」與「勢」實在是一體之兩面，一靜一動，寓動於靜，木石原本是靜止的，不去動它，永遠不會產生動力，但放置在千仞高山上，滾動而下，運動速度增大，其威力就無法遏止了，所以「勢」之運用，全看將帥如何去創造了。

CHAPTER 6

STRENGTH AND WEAKNESS

「虛實」篇主要在說明作戰貴立於主動地位，避實擊虛，取敵人之弱點，而自己則深藏不露，無懈可擊。事實上，無論再強大的軍旅都會有強有力的部份和較為軟弱的部份，這就是「虛實」，善用兵者，一定乘敵之弱；用我之強，以我之強；制敵之弱，此即「致人而不致於人」。

所謂「致人」，是依我的意思支配敵人，我之所欲，敵人雖不情願，也不得不往

而受我之牽制不能往，這就是孫所說的：「能使敵自至者，利之也；能使敵不得至者，害之也。」

所謂「不致於人」，即處處不受敵之支配，進退自如，避敵之實，擊敵之虛，敵不能禦，也不能迫我

，就是：「出其所不趨，趨其所不意。」

CONTROL OTHERS WITHOUT BEING CONTROLLED

WHOEVER ARRIVES AT THE BATTLEFIELD FIRST WILL BE AT EASE AND IN A POSITION TO TAKE THE INITIATIVE.

THE LATECOMER WILL HAVE TO RUSH TO MEET THE ENEMY ON THE BATTLEFIELD AND THUS WILL BE TIRED AND AT A DISADVANTAGE.

THE ABLE MILITARY COMMANDER CONTROLS THE ENEMY AND IS NOT CONTROLLED BY THE ENEMY.

COME ON! COME ON!

76

ONE WHO WANTS TO GET THE ENEMY TO HIS CHOICE OF BATTLEFIELDS ENTICES HIM WITH AN APPARENT ADVANTAGE.

ONE WHO WANTS TO KEEP THE ENEMY AWAY THREATENS HIM WITH FORCE.

WHEN THE ENEMY WANTS TO SLOW DOWN, KEEP HIM RUNNING; WHEN HE WANTS TO EAT, KEEP HIM HUNGRY; WHEN HE WANTS TO REST, MAKE HIM MOVE.

「致人而不致於人」含有兩個原則，一是主動；一是機動。要支配敵人，必處處主動；要不受制於敵人，必時時機動，以主動配合機動，搶先部署有利地位，誘使敵人進入我所預定的決戰地點，或使敵人誤認我力量強大，不敢來犯，這就是主動和機動的運用。

77

「我專敵分」是集中原則的運用，所謂「集中」，乃是在一定時間、空間內，將最大戰力放在決勝點上，對敵人實施決定性的打擊，以發揮我方之絕對優勢。但欲達到此一目的，必先分散敵人力量，也就是讓敵人不能集中，故要用佯攻、牽制等等手段，使敵人備多力分，而受制於我。

CONCENTRATION AGAINST FRAGMENTATION

BY EMPLOYING DIVERSIONARY TACTICS AND KEEPING YOUR REAL CIRCUMSTANCES HIDDEN, YOU CAN FOOL THE ENEMY IN REGARD TO YOUR ACTUAL SIZE AND LOCATION, THEREBY FORCING THE ENEMY TO SPREAD OUT. IN THIS WAY, THE ENEMY'S FORCES WILL BE DIVIDED, WHILE YOUR OWN REMAIN CONCENTRATED.

HERE'S MY MAIN FORCE!

I CONCENTRATE MY POWER IN ONE PLACE, WHILE THE ENEMY'S IS FRAGMENTED IN TEN PLACES. THIS WAY, I HAVE A TENFOLD ADVANTAGE.

BY OUTNUMBERING THE ENEMY, HE IS RENDERED WEAK AND EASY TO CONTROL.

I CAN'T WIN WITH THIS FRAGMENTATION....

AT A SPECIFIED TIME AND IN A SPECIFIED PLACE, CONCENTRATION AGAINST FRAGMENTATION IS EXERTING THE GREATEST POWER AT A POINT OF CERTAIN VICTORY, THUS STRIKING A DECISIVE BLOW AGAINST THE ENEMY AND GIVING YOU CERTAIN SUPERIORITY.

LIKE WATER

THE PRINCIPLE FOR DEPLOYING SOLDIERS IS TO EMULATE WATER. WATER FLOWS FROM HIGHER GROUND TO LOWER GROUND;

AND THE RULE FOR WAGING WAR IS TO AVOID STRENGTHS AND STRIKE AT WEAKNESSES.

WATER CHANGES COURSE ACCORDING TO TERRAIN;

AND IN MILITARY DEPLOYMENT, YOU WANT TO CHANGE YOUR COURSE TOWARD VICTORY ACCORDING TO THE ENEMY'S CHANGING CIRCUMSTANCES, CONFRONTING HIM AND DEFEATING HIM.

水本沒有一定的形，水因不同之容器而呈現不同的形狀，水只有不變的性質而無外在形體，用兵亦復如此，有不變的原則，而無固定方法，以水喻兵，可謂千古名言。

79

水形象水」的本義。

水原本是至柔之物，但是一旦化為激流，則可以滾滾滔滔，有驚人力量，所以水之柔，是水的本性；水之強，是一定的「勢」造就成的。水在靜態的時候是柔；使之激盪，就轉弱為強，所以用兵應注意「兵

THERE ARE NO ABSOLUTE PRECEPTS FOR WAGING WAR, JUST AS WATER DOES NOT HAVE ONLY ONE SHAPE. HE IS INDEED A GODLIKE GENERAL WHO CAN ADAPT TO THE CHANGING CONDITIONS OF A WAR AND THEREBY GAIN VICTORY.

DEPLOYING FORCES IS LIKE THE TRANSFORMATIONS AMONG THE FIVE ELEMENTS—METAL, WOOD, WATER, FIRE, AND EARTH—ALTERNATELY ARISING AND GIVING WAY, NOT CONCERNED WITH WHICH ONE IS AT A TEMPORARY ADVANTAGE.

SPRING, SUMMER, FALL, AND WINTER TAKE TURNS ONE AFTER THE OTHER;

SOME DAYS ARE LONG AND OTHERS SHORT;

THE MOON WAXES AND WANES.

THE PRINCIPLE OF DEPLOYING FORCES IS THAT THERE ARE NO CERTAIN METHODS, JUST LIKE FLOWING WATER, WHICH IS CONSTANTLY CHANGING DIRECTION. SO THERE ARE NO CERTAIN RULES FOR MILITARY DEPLOYMENT—JUST AVOID STRENGTHS AND STRIKE AT WEAKNESSES. ALTERNATE YOUR TACTICS FROM SURPRISE TO FRONTAL CONFRONTATIONS AND BACK, ACCORDING TO THE ENEMY'S CIRCUMSTANCES.

水一定順地勢向低流，用兵亦必順應敵情而向其虛弱處進攻，敵之弱即襯托出我之強，這就是乘其弱勢而用我之強勢。弱和強是由比較得來的，我「專」敵「分」，我才顯得強大，所以能掌握形勢，善用虛實，自然用兵如神了。

81

「軍爭」篇主要在說明會戰要領。兩軍對峙到最後，勢必用會戰的手段，一決勝負。孫子認為會戰最難的就是如何化迂迴曲折之遠路為直線近路，如何化種種不利的情況為有利情況，因為迂迴曲折的作戰路線往往是敵人期待性最小，抵抗力最弱的路線，可收出奇制勝之效。

CHAPTER 7

MANEUVER

MAKE THE CROOKED STRAIGHT

THE CORRECT METHOD OF MANIPULATING FORCES IS TO STRUGGLE WITH THE ENEMY AT THE FRONT LINES FOR ADVANTAGES THAT CAN LEAD TO VICTORY, SUCH AS:

HOW TO TURN THE LONG DISTANCE OF A CROOKED ROAD INTO THE SHORT DISTANCE OF A STRAIGHT ROAD, THEREBY ARRIVING AT THE BATTLEFIELD BEFORE THE ENEMY,

AND HOW TO TURN ALL KINDS OF DISADVANTAGES INTO ADVANTAGES.

WHEN STRUGGLING FOR ADVANTAGES THAT CAN LEAD TO VICTORY, THERE ARE BENEFICIAL ASPECTS AS WELL AS DANGEROUS ASPECTS.

HEE-HEE-HEE...

孫子說：「軍爭之難者，以迂為直，以患為利。」「迂」與「直」相反；「患」與「利」相背，「直」不可得即以「迂」取之；「利」不可得即以趨「患」之方法誘敵，冀由小害得大利，以迂迴方式得機先，所以其中利害關係，必須慎重考量。

83

會戰是大兵團作戰，雙方都希望在一定的時間內，集結足夠的兵力，因此速度成為發揮機動力量的要件。古代道路不良，如人馬輜重一齊行動，則速度必遲緩，如棄輜重而急行軍，速度雖快，能集結之兵力必相對減少，戰鬥力亦隨之降低；有速度而無力量，如強弩之末，是用兵大忌。

ADVANTAGE AND DISADVANTAGE

IF THE ENTIRE ARMY SETS OUT TOGETHER, WITH MEN, HORSES, AND CARTS, THE GOING WILL SURELY BE SLOW.

AND ALTHOUGH IT WOULD BE SWIFTER IF THE CARTS AND EQUIPMENT WERE LEFT BEHIND, THEY COULD EASILY BE CAPTURED BY THE ENEMY.

HA-HA-HA. NOW THAT WE HAVE THE ENEMY'S SUPPLIES, WE'LL WIN FOR SURE.

EEK!

FURTHERMORE, IF YOU ATTEMPT TO MAKE UP TIME BY MARCHING ALL DAY AND ALL NIGHT WITH LIGHT PACKS, YOU MAY BE ABLE TO INCREASE YOUR DISTANCE BY TWENTY-SOME MILES A DAY,

BUT THE ARMY WILL BE DISPERSED BECAUSE THE STRONGER ONES WILL GET OUT AHEAD WHILE THE EXHAUSTED ONES FALL BEHIND. IF THIS IS THE CASE, ONLY ONE TENTH OF YOUR ARMY WILL BE ABLE TO MAKE A HASTY ARRIVAL AT THE BATTLEFIELD,

AND ONCE THEY ARRIVE THERE, THEY WILL SURELY BE DEFEATED. THERE IS ALSO THE POSSIBILITY THAT, IN THE DEFEAT, THE COMMANDERS WILL BE CAPTURED.

THEREFORE, IF IT IS NOT BACKED UP BY TRANSPORT WAGONS, THE ARMY WILL NOT SURVIVE.

IF THERE ARE NO SUPPLIES AND PROVISIONS, THE ARMY WILL NOT SURVIVE; IF THERE IS NO STORE OF EQUIPMENT, THE ARMY WILL NOT SURVIVE.

大兵團運動，後勤補給至為重要，如發生問題，後果不堪設想，孫子說：「軍無輜重則亡；無糧食則亡；無委積則亡。」可見軍旅的戰力與後勤補給有密切關係，將帥不能只求快速運動，而忽略了後勤的補給能力。

85

作戰區域如在國境之外，則第三國的態度，非常重要，軍旅出征，本身接壤之鄰國，亦可影響大局，所以孫子注意「豫交」。此外，國境外作戰，「地形」及「鄉導」亦非常需要瞭解，如不能善用「地形」和「鄉導」，既不能行軍，更無法戰鬥了。

IN ADDITION, IF YOU DO NOT UNDERSTAND THE INTENTIONS OF FOREIGN GOVERNMENTS, YOU WILL NOT BE ABLE TO BUILD ALLIANCES WITH THEM.

IF YOU DO NOT UNDERSTAND THE TERRAIN OF MOUNTAINS, FORESTS, HAZARDOUS AREAS, MARSHES, AND SWAMPS, YOU WILL NOT BE ABLE TO MOVE YOUR TROOPS AND ENGAGE IN WAR.

IF YOU CANNOT EMPLOY THE LOCALS AS GUIDES, YOU WILL NOT BE ABLE TO OBTAIN THE ADVANTAGES THAT THE TERRAIN HAS TO OFFER.

WIND,
FOREST,
FIRE,
MOUNTAIN

WHEN WAGING WAR, YOU MUST EMPLOY CUNNING TACTICS AND MULTIPLE TRANSFORMATIONS IN ORDER TO SUCCEED.

YOU MUST JUDGE WHETHER OR NOT SOMETHING IS ADVANTAGEOUS BEFORE YOU ACT.

YOU MUST DECIDE WHETHER TO CONCENTRATE YOUR TROOPS OR DIVIDE THEM ACCORDING TO CHANGING CIRCUMSTANCES.

孫子對將帥用兵，舉出六個準則；「疾如風」、「徐如林」、「侵掠如火」、「不動如山」、「難知如陰」、「動如雷霆」。這是說軍旅行動要快如「風」，靜止時如「林」木無語；進攻時如烈「火」燎原；防守時如「山」岳難撼；隱藏時如「陰」雲遮天；快速發動時如迅「雷」不及掩耳。

日本戰國時代大將軍；也是甲卅兵學之祖的武田信玄最欽服孫子這幾句話，他把「疾如風、徐如林、侵掠如火、不動如山」四句話繡在軍旗上，做為號誌，以後「風林火山」四字就成為武田信玄的代表。

WIND

WHEN MOVING, YOU MUST BE FLEET LIKE THE WIND.

FOREST

WHEN STOPPING, YOU MUST BE STILL LIKE THE TREES IN A FOREST.

FIRE

WHEN ATTACKING, YOU MUST BE FEROCIOUS LIKE THE SEARING FLAMES OF A FIRE.

MOUNTAIN

WHEN DEFENDING, YOU MUST BE IMMOVABLE LIKE A MOUNTAIN.

LIGHTNING

WHEN ADVANCING, YOU MUST BE SUDDEN LIKE LIGHTNING, ALLOWING THE ENEMY NO CHANCE FOR RETREAT.

CLOUDS

WHEN HIDING, YOU MUST COMPLETELY DISAPPEAR, AS THOUGH BEHIND DARK CLOUDS.

WHEN ENGAGING IN WARFARE, YOU SHOULD BASE YOUR ACTIONS ON THE CHANGING CIRCUMSTANCES OF THE ENEMY. CONSIDER THE CHANGES, TAKE ADVANTAGE OF OPPORTUNITIES, AND GAIN VICTORY THROUGH THE ENEMY. IF YOU CAN BE LIKE THESE SIX THINGS— WIND, FOREST, FIRE, MOUNTAIN, CLOUD, AND LIGHTNING— VICTORY WILL BE YOURS.

「風、林、火、山、陰、雷」是孫子對軍旅作戰之要求，如能確實做到，則必定是一支常勝勁旅，不過這必須靠平時不斷的嚴格訓練，尤其要具備嚴整的軍紀，才能收如臂使指，號令齊一之效。

89

「九變」篇主要在說明將帥指揮軍旅應注意之事項。將帥為軍旅之中樞，負作戰成敗之重任，因此切不能以一己之好惡，任性行事，應考慮各種狀況，做成適當判斷，同時以冷靜理智的思考方式，以避免錯誤的決定。

CHAPTER 8

ALTERNATIVES

ALTERNATIVES

SUNZI SAID:

IN COMMANDING TROOPS, THE GENERAL RECEIVES THE ORDER FROM THE SOVEREIGN, THE PEOPLE ARE CONSCRIPTED, AND AN ARMY IS FORMED....

DO NOT BIVOUAC ON HAZARDOUS TERRAIN:

AT INTERSECTING TERRITORIES, ALLY WITH THE NEIGHBORING COUNTRIES;

DO NOT LINGER IN TERRAIN THAT SEPARATES YOU FROM YOUR SUPPLIES;

「九變」的解釋，歷來各家並不一致，大體可分為兩種。一是把「九」看做實數，即孫子說的：「圮地無舍、衢地合交、絕地無留、圍地則謀、死地則戰、途有所不由、軍有所不擊、城有所不攻、地有所不爭、君命有所不受」。一是把「九」看成虛數，「九變」即千變萬化之意。

孫子特別重視地形，自「軍爭」、「九變」到「行軍」、「地形」、「九地」各篇，都談到地形地物的利用，而且愈講愈詳細，對每一種地形都從戰略及戰術方面加以分析，因此本篇中所涉及的五種地形：「圯地」、「衢地」、「絕地」、「圍地」、「死地」，在「九地」篇中，都有很詳細的說明。

IN ENCLOSED GROUND, SEEK ESCAPE;

IN DESPERATE GROUND, FIGHT;

SOME ROADS ARE NOT TO BE TRAVERSED;

SOME ARMIES ARE NOT TO BE ENGAGED;

LET THEM GO. WE'LL CONCENTRATE OUR ATTACK ELSEWHERE.

SOME CITIES ARE NOT TO BE STORMED;

WE'LL SKIP THE CITY AND DIRECTLY ATTACK THEIR MAJOR ENCAMPMENT.

SOME BATTLEFIELDS ARE TO BE FORGONE;

WE'LL SKIP THAT AREA AND STRIKE HERE WITH ALL OUR STRENGTH.

SOME OF THE SOVEREIGN'S ORDERS ARE TO BE IGNORED;

IF YOUR ORDERS ARE CONTRARY TO ULTIMATE VICTORY, I AM FORCED TO DISOBEY.

IF A COMMANDER TAKES INTO ACCOUNT THE BENEFITS OF THESE ALTERNATIVES, THEN HE CAN BE SAID TO UNDERSTAND WARFARE.

IF HE DOES NOT, THEN, EVEN THOUGH HE MAY UNDERSTAND TERRAIN, HE WILL NOT BE ABLE TO TAKE ADVANTAGE OF IT. IF IN MANAGING HIS FORCES HE CANNOT ADJUST TO CHANGING SITUATIONS, EVEN THOUGH HE MAY UNDERSTAND THE BENEFITS TO BE GAINED THROUGH TERRAIN, HE WILL NOT BE ABLE TO FULLY UTILIZE HIS FORCES.

至於「途有所不由，軍有所不擊，城有所不攻，地有所不爭，君命有所不受。」則是五種不同情況下的通變，前四項著眼於戰術及戰略的考量，至於「君命不受」，乃是強調將帥把握戰機，並非事事可以不受君命，「不受命」是為了軍旅及國家安全，是一時權變，並不是隨便抗命，否則就成為叛逆，絕非孫子所說的良將了。

93

94

THEREFORE, ACCORDING TO THE PRINCIPLES AND TACTICS OF WARFARE, DO NOT EXPECT THE ENEMY NOT TO COME. INSTEAD, BE IN COMPLETE MILITARY READINESS.

DO NOT EXPECT THE ENEMY NOT TO ATTACK. INSTEAD, ASSURE YOURSELF THAT THE ENEMY WOULD NOT BE SUCCESSFUL IN THE EVENT OF AN ATTACK.

THERE ARE FIVE PERSONAL TRAITS THAT ARE DANGEROUS IN A COMMANDER:

I. HE WHO IS INTENT ON DYING CAN BE MURDERED.
II. HE WHO IS INTENT ON LIVING CAN BE CAPTURED.
III. HE WHO IS QUICK TO ANGER CAN BE INSULTED.
IV. HE WHO IS SELF-CONSCIOUS CAN BE HUMILIATED.
V. HE WHO IS COMPASSIONATE CAN BE TROUBLED.

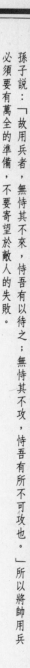

孫子說：「故用兵者，無恃其不來，恃吾有以待之；無恃其不攻，恃吾有所不可攻也。」所以將帥用兵必須要有萬全的準備，不要寄望於敵人的失敗。

95

將帥有五項最危險的事：①只知死拼，如暴虎馮河，就可能遭敵人所殺；②貪生怕死，臨陣畏怯，就可能遭敵俘虜。

I. HE WHO UNDERSTANDS ONLY RESOLUTION THROUGH VIOLENCE IS LIKELY TO BE CUT DOWN BY THE ENEMY.

II. HE WHO FEARS DEATH AND IS AFRAID IN THE FACE OF BATTLE IS LIKELY TO BE CAPTURED BY THE ENEMY.

「行軍」篇主要在說明軍旅在山地、河川、沼澤、平陸等四種地形的用兵法則，以及三十三種觀察敵人虛實的方法。古代交通不便，部隊行進的阻礙重重，因此作戰時必須因地制宜，充分利用各種地形的特性。同時，大部隊運動時，必有一些無法隱藏的跡象，觀察這些跡象，便可判斷敵人虛實，對敵情研判有極大幫助。

CHAPTER 9

ON THE MARCH

98

DEPLOYMENT

SUNZI SAID:

WHEN DEPLOYING TROOPS AND OBSERVING THE ENEMY, YOU SHOULD TAKE INTO ACCOUNT THE FOLLOWING POINTS:

WHEN TRAVERSING MOUNTAINS, FOLLOW THE VALLEY FLOORS:

LOOK FOR PLACES SUITABLE TO ATTACK OR DEFEND, AS WELL AS HIGH PLACES THAT ARE SUITABLE FOR STATIONING TROOPS.

IF THE ENEMY IS THE FIRST TO GAIN THE HIGH GROUND, DO NOT COMMENCE A FRONTAL ASSAULT. THESE ARE THE PRINCIPLES OF DEPLOYING TROOPS IN A MOUNTAINOUS AREA.

關於「處山之軍」（山地作戰），孫子主張要「絕山依谷，視生處高」，即靠近山谷前進，同時佔據制高點。依山谷進軍的好處是谷內的水草可以補充人馬體力，佔據制高點則是便於鳥瞰敵人，保持警戒。但當敵人已先佔高地時，則不要勉強仰攻，須設法迂迴。

99

關於「處水上之軍」（河川戰），孫子認為部隊在渡河之前和渡河之後，其集結位置要與河川保持適當距離，以利兵力之機動。如敵人渡河向我攻擊，不要迎擊於水中，等其半渡時，其兵力分散在近岸、河中、遠岸時，才發動攻擊，效果最大。

WHEN FORDING A RIVER, CROSS QUICKLY AND DISTANCE YOURSELF FROM IT, LEST THE ENEMY TAKE ADVANTAGE OF THE SITUATION;

IF THE ENEMY CROSSES A RIVER IN THE COURSE OF THEIR ATTACK, DO NOT ENTER THE WATER TO ENGAGE THEM;

NOT YET ...

WAIT UNTIL THEY ARE HALF ACROSS AND HALF IN THE WATER, THEN ATTACK.

ATTACK!

IF ANTICIPATING ENGAGEMENT WITH THE ENEMY, DO NOT ENGAGE FROM A RIVERBANK;

關於「處斥澤之軍」（沼澤作戰），孫子認為這種地形本不宜作戰，最好「亟去勿留」，如果一定要作戰時，必須靠近水草而且背後有樹林倚托，因為有樹林的地區，土質較密實，不會深陷泥濘。

101

孫子說：「敵近而靜者，恃其險也；遠而挑戰者，欲人之進也；其所居易者，利也。」這是從敵人所居營舍駐地的位置，觀察其動靜。

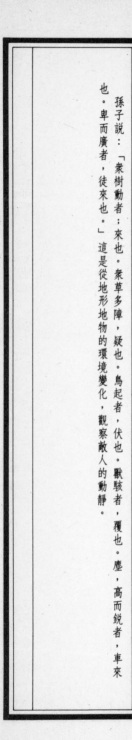

孫子説：「辭卑而益備者，進也。辭強而進驅者，退也。」「輕車先出其側者，陣也。」「無約而請和者，謀也。」這些都是從敵方的行動上觀察，以判斷其下一步的動作。

「地形」篇主要在說明「通」、「挂」、「支」、「隘」、「險」、「遠」等六種地形的利用，以及將帥因措置失當，以致犯了「走」、「弛」、「陷」、「崩」、「亂」、「北」六種錯誤的情形。

CHAPTER 10

TERRAIN

所謂「通形」是平易開闊，四通八達、敵我均可以往來的地形，在這種地形作戰，要先佔領高地，而且確保補給線的暢通，以便於糧草的輸送。

107

OBSTRUCTED TERRAIN

TERRAIN ON WHICH YOU CAN EASILY ADVANCE BUT NOT RETREAT IS CALLED "OBSTRUCTED."

WHEN DOING BATTLE ON THIS KIND OF TERRAIN, YOU CAN WIN IF YOU ATTACK WHILE THE ENEMY IS STILL UNPREPARED. IF YOU ATTACK WHEN THE ENEMY IS PREPARED, YOU WILL NOT WIN ...

AND RETREAT WILL BE DIFFICULT. IN THIS WAY, IT WILL BE DISADVANTAGEOUS.

TERRAIN ON WHICH IT IS DIFFICULT FOR EITHER SIDE TO ADVANCE IS CALLED "RESTRICTED."

RESTRICTED TERRAIN

「挂形」是容易進；不易退的地形，如果敵人有備，斷我退路，就非常不利。「支形」則是我軍與敵軍之間有暴露的地段，如潮泊、河川、平原等，誰先出擊，誰就暴露身形，所以不可先出，要誘使敵人離開險要，才集中主力攻擊。

ON THIS KIND OF TERRAIN, EVEN IF THE ENEMY ENTICES YOU, DO NOT ADVANCE. INSTEAD, RETREAT, FORCING HIM TO FOLLOW ...

WAIT UNTIL HALF OF THEM ARE THROUGH, THEN TURN AND ATTACK. IN THIS WAY, IT WILL BE ADVANTAGEOUS.

BE THE FIRST TO STAND THE CONSTRICTED GROUND. ESTABLISH A DEFENSE THERE AND AWAIT THE ENEMY.

CONSTRICTED TERRAIN

IF HE TAKES THE CONSTRICTED GROUND FIRST AND ESTABLISHES A DEFENSE, DO NOT FORCE AN ATTACK.

IF HE TAKES THE CONSTRICTED GROUND AND DOES NOT ESTABLISH A DEFENSE, YOU MAY CONSIDER ATTACKING.

所謂「隘形」，是指兩山夾峙之隘道、隘口，在這種地形作戰，應先佔隘口，沿隘道做縱深佈署，如敵軍先佔隘口，不要冒險去攻擊，但是如敵軍守在隘道中間，隘口防守薄弱，則可發動攻擊，這就是孫子說的「盈而勿從，不盈而從之。」

109

ON PRECIPITOUS TERRAIN, FIRST STAND AT THE ESSENTIAL POINTS OF TRANSIT AND TAKE THE HIGH GROUND, WHERE YOU WILL AWAIT THE ENEMY.

PRECIPITOUS TERRAIN

IF THE ENEMY GETS TO THESE PLACES FIRST, LEAD YOUR TROOPS AWAY. DO NOT RECKLESSLY ATTACK.

TURN BACK!

DISTANT TERRAIN

"DISTANT" TERRAIN REFERS TO BOTH SIDES BEING FAR AWAY FROM EACH OTHER. ON THIS KIND OF TERRAIN, IF THE FORCES ARE EQUAL, IT IS DIFFICULT FOR EITHER SIDE TO WIN DECISIVELY.

THESE ARE THE SIX KINDS OF TERRAIN AND THE PRINCIPLES FOR USING THEM CORRECTLY. IT IS THE PRIMARY RESPONSIBILITY OF THE GENERAL TO TAKE THEM INTO CAREFUL CONSIDERATION.

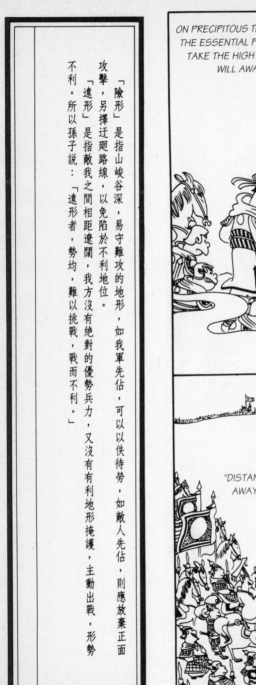

「險形」是指山峻谷深，易守難攻的地形，如我軍先佔，可以以佚待勞，如敵人先佔，則應放棄正面攻擊，另擇迂迴路線，以免陷於不利地位。

「遠形」是指敵我之間相距遼闊，我方沒有絕對的優勢兵力，又沒有有利地形掩護，主動出戰，形勢不利。所以孫子說：「遠形者，勢均，難以挑戰，戰而不利。」

「六敗」不是地形之害而是人為錯誤，所以孫子說：「凡此六者，敗之道也。將之至任，不可不察也。」又說：「凡此六者，非天地之災，將之過也。」主要是提醒將帥要做正確的判斷，不要做錯誤的決定。

不過「六敗」之中，「走」、「北」兩項，確屬將帥的判斷正確與否，其餘「弛」、「陷」、「崩」、「亂」四項，都與平素訓練、號令紀律有關，所以孫子再三強調：「厚而不能使、愛而不能令、亂而不能治，譬若驕子，不可用也。」

WHEN THE HIGH-RANKING OFFICERS DOMINATE AND RECKLESSLY ATTACK, WITH THE COMMANDER UNABLE TO CONTROL THEM, THIS IS CALLED "COLLAPSE."

DO NOT ATTACK!

I'M NO COWARD LIKE YOU ARE!

IF THE COMMANDER IS NOT STRICT, IS NOT SKILLED IN TRAINING HIS TROOPS, THE TROOPS HAVE NO DISCIPLINE, AND BATTLE DEPLOYMENT IS DISORGANIZED, THIS IS CALLED "CHAOS."

FALL IN!

TAKE A HIKE.

IF THE COMMANDER DOES NOT KNOW HOW TO EVALUATE THE ENEMY, SETTING A SMALL FORCE AGAINST A LARGER OR A WEAK FORCE AGAINST A STRONGER, OR IF HE DOES NOT EMPLOY SHOCK TROOPS IN THE FRONT RANKS, THIS IS CALLED CERTAIN "DEFEAT."

THESE ARE THE SIX KINDS OF DEFEAT. IT IS THE PRIMARY RESPONSIBILITY OF THE GENERAL TO TAKE THEM INTO CAREFUL CONSIDERATION.

IT'S ALL MY FAULT THAT WE WERE DEFEATED!

A GREAT GENERAL IS A NATIONAL TREASURE

TERRAIN IS AN IMPORTANT FACTOR THAT CAN BE OF HELP IN WAGING WAR. IF YOU CAN USE IT AGAINST THE ENEMY, YOU ARE ASSURED VICTORY, AND IF YOU CANNOT, DEFEAT IS CERTAIN.

VICTORY IS CERTAIN! ALL FORCES ATTACK!

IF A GENERAL IS CERTAIN OF VICTORY, HE SHOULD RELENTLESSLY ATTACK UNTIL VICTORY IS GAINED. IF NOT, HE SHOULD DISCONTINUE WAGING WAR.

THE GENERAL MAY TEMPORARILY DISREGARD THE SOVEREIGN'S ORDERS.

IF DEFEAT IS CERTAIN, WE SHOULD NOT FIGHT!

I WANT A FIGHT!

THE GREAT GENERAL ADVANCES WITHOUT SEEKING RECOGNITION AND RETREATS WITHOUT SHIRKING RESPONSIBILITY. HE ACTS ONLY FOR THE BENEFIT OF THE PEOPLE. IN THIS WAY, HE IS A NATIONAL TREASURE.

THE BEST KIND OF GENERAL IS ONE WHO DOES NOT SEEK FAME OR AVOID BLAME AND WHO TAKES THE PROTECTION OF THE PEOPLE AS HIS HIGHEST PRIORITY.

孫子在本篇又再度說明將帥之重要性，他認為將帥能「進不求名、退不避罪，唯民是保，而利於至，」這樣子的將帥才是「國之寶也」。

113

「九地」篇主要說明九種戰略地形：「散地」、「輕地」、「爭地」、「交地」、「衢地」、「重地」、「圮地」、「圍地」、「死地」等，以及交戰於國境之內和交戰於國境之外的用兵原則。「九地」是孫子十三篇中最長的一篇，計一千餘字，可以說是對「九變」、「行軍」、「地形」等，有關戰場作戰地形利用的總結。

CHAPTER 11

GROUND

STRATEGIES OF GROUND

ACCORDING TO THE PRINCIPLES AND TACTICS OF WARFARE, THERE ARE NINE KINDS OF GROUND: DISPERSIVE, SHALLOW, CONTENTIOUS, COMMUNICATING, PIVOTAL, DEEP, HAZARDOUS, ENCIRCLED, AND MORTAL.

IF YOUR ARMY IS BATTLING IN YOUR OWN TERRITORY, THIS IS CALLED "DISPERSIVE GROUND."

IF YOU ENTER A SHORT DISTANCE ACROSS THE BORDER, THIS IS CALLED "SHALLOW GROUND."

WHEN YOU AND THE ENEMY HAVE BOTH GAINED THE SAME ADVANTAGEOUS POSITION, THIS IS CALLED "CONTENTIOUS GROUND."

WHEN YOU CAN ADVANCE TOWARD THE ENEMY AND THE ENEMY CAN ADVANCE TOWARD YOU, THIS IS CALLED "COMMUNICATING GROUND."

孫子說「散地無戰」，並非不抵抗之意，而是認為久戰於本國之內，士卒思鄉顧家，易於離散，所以「無戰」是不宜做大規模的會戰。而且，大戰於國境內，鄉里破壞很大，也不是最好的選擇。必不得已，非戰不可時，亦不必急於決戰，可誘敵深入，使敵人力量分散，再伺機決戰。所以孫子說的「無戰」，實含有多種意義。

115

至於「爭地」、「交地」、「衢地」三者，都是屬於戰略目標，「爭地」是兵家必爭之地；「交地」是交通孔道；「衢地」是樞紐地區，所以皆不能單憑武力奪取，必佐以外交手段，用「伐謀」、「伐交」的方法取得控制權。

WHEN YOU HAVE OCCUPIED A STRATEGIC AREA FROM WHICH YOU CAN CONTROL THE OTHER STATES, THIS IS CALLED "PIVOTAL GROUND."

WHEN YOU ARE FAR INSIDE THE ENEMY'S TERRITORY AND HAVE PASSED SEVERAL TOWNS AND CITIES, THIS IS CALLED "DEEP GROUND."

WHEN YOU ARE IN THE MOUNTAINS, A FOREST, ON DANGEROUS TERRAIN, OR IN A SWAMP OR MARSH, THIS IS CALLED "HAZARDOUS GROUND."

WHEN YOU ENTER A PASSAGEWAY THAT IS NARROW, WHERE THE ROAD OF RETREAT IS LONG OR WHERE YOU CAN BE ATTACKED FROM ALL SIDES, THIS IS CALLED "ENCIRCLED GROUND."

WHEN YOU HAVE NO CHOICE BUT TO FIGHT OR DIE, THIS IS CALLED "MORTAL GROUND."

116

ON DISPERSIVE GROUND, DO NOT ENGAGE THE ENEMY RIGHT AWAY. BEFORE ATTACKING, ENTICE THE ENEMY DEEPER INTO YOUR OWN TERRITORY.

HEE HEE...

ON SHALLOW GROUND, YOU SHOULD NOT HOLD BACK BUT CONTINUE FIGHTING ON.

IN REGARD TO CONTENTIOUS GROUND, YOU MUST OCCUPY IT FIRST. IF THE ENEMY OCCUPIES IT, DO NOT ATTACK.

WHEN ON COMMUNICATING GROUND, BE SURE TO MAINTAIN YOUR LINES OF SUPPLY AND INFORMATION.

「輕地」是去國不遠的地區，士卒畏戰思鄉的心理，可能仍然存在，所以孫子說「輕地無止」，以免銳氣消失。不過就另一方面來看，如果沒有深入敵境的打算，亦可輕易退回國境，所以孫子也說：「合於利而動，不合於利而止。」

117

至於「重地」、「圯地」、「圍地」、「死地」，都是深入敵境之後的情形。其中孫子最重視「死地」，他除說：「死地則戰」外，還強調：「投之亡地然後存，陷之死地然後生」，以及「死地，吾將予之不活。」這是針對士卒的戰場心理而發的，士卒在極端困阨險要的境地中，求生之欲油然而生，自然能發揮勇氣，死中求生。

WHEN YOU ARE ON PIVOTAL GROUND, YOU ARE FREE TO BEGIN DIPLOMATIC NEGOTIATIONS.

WHEN ON DEEP GROUND, PLUNDER FOR PROVISIONS.

LET'S GO! THIS IS WHERE WE ARE MOST VULNERABLE!

WHEN ON HAZARDOUS GROUND, MAKE HASTE TO GET OUT OF IT.

WHEN ON ENCIRCLED GROUND, DEVISE A STRATEGY TO FREE YOURSELF.

WHEN ON MORTAL GROUND, FIGHT TOOTH AND NAIL.

DIVIDING THE ENEMY

EVER SINCE ANCIENT TIMES, AN ABLE MILITARY COMMANDER HAS KEPT THE ENEMY FROM PROTECTING BOTH HIS FRONT AND REAR.

HE WOULD CUT OFF THE SMALLER FORCES FROM THE LARGER, SO THAT THEY WOULD BE ISOLATED AND COULD NOT COME TO EACH OTHER'S AID.

HE WOULD KEEP THEM FROM CHANGING POSITION OR CONCENTRATING THEIR STRENGTH IN ATTACK.

ONLY ACT WHEN IN AN ADVANTAGEOUS POSITION; AND WHEN IN A DISADVANTAGEOUS POSITION, DON'T DO ANYTHING RASH.

「內線作戰」是在中央位置，面對兩個或兩個以上方向，向居中央位置的敵人發動攻擊。

「內線作戰」是在敵人分進而尚未合擊時，各個擊破；「外線作戰」則是由不同方向向目標集中，分進合擊，在同一時間內，集中優勢力量在一個決戰點上，兩者之優劣，難以一言蔽之，必須由將帥下決心，做判斷。

上方向之來敵作戰；「外線作戰」則是從兩個或兩個以

119

孫子說：「是故始如處女，敵人開戶、後如脫兔，敵不及拒。」主要意旨在說明作戰必求迅速，在敵人料想不到的時間、地點、發動優勢兵力，全面攻擊，一舉殲滅，這非靠「迅速」不可。

THE ARMY OF THE SUPREME SOVEREIGN

ONE WHO DOES NOT UNDERSTAND INTERNATIONAL AFFAIRS WILL NOT BE ABLE TO MAKE EFFECTIVE USE OF DIPLOMATIC RELATIONS.

SORRY, BUT OUR COUNTRY'S POLICY HAS SUDDENLY CHANGED. MY APOLOGIES ...

ONE WHO IS NOT FAMILIAR WITH THE GEOGRAPHY OF MOUNTAINS, FORESTS, SWAMPS, MARSHES, AND OTHER HAZARDOUS TERRAIN WILL NOT BE ABLE TO LEAD TROOPS INTO BATTLE.

ONE WHO DOES NOT UTILIZE THE LOCALS AS GUIDES WILL NOT BE ABLE TO USE THE TERRAIN TO HIS ADVANTAGE.

IF A GENERAL LACKS ONE OF THE ABOVE CHARACTERISTICS, HIS ARMY CANNOT BE CALLED THE ARMY OF THE SUPREME SOVEREIGN.

戰爭是威勢與力量的決戰，孫子是從這個角度來觀察，所以他說：「夫霸王之兵，伐大國，則其眾不得聚，威加於敵，則其交不得合。」這是政治與軍事力量的展示，但畢竟是霸道，而非王道。孫子在十三篇之首的「始計」中，以及其他各篇裡，均一再談到「修道保法」，可見他並不是一個霸道的擁護者，孫子只是就兵論兵，以用兵的威勢力量做一總結而已。

121

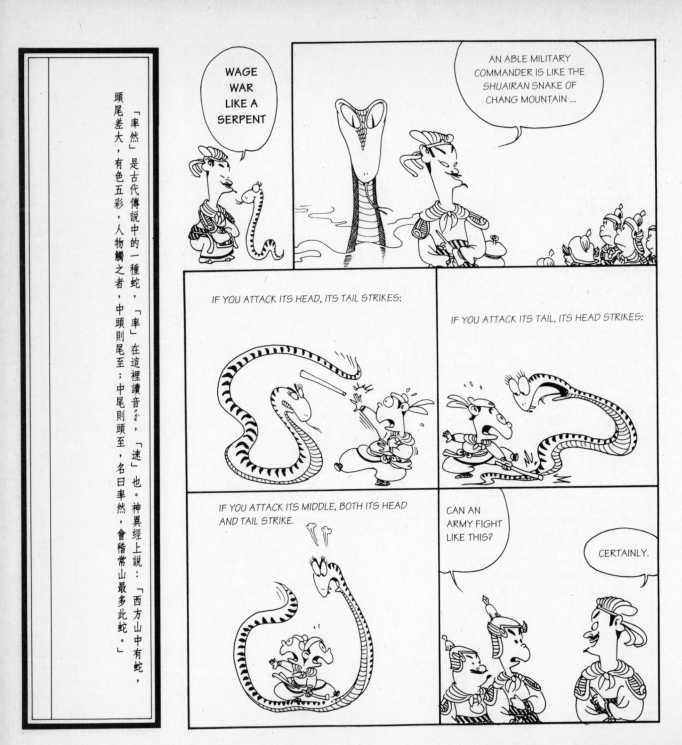

「率然」是古代傳説中的一種蛇，「率」在這裡讀音ㄕㄨㄞˋ，「速」也。神異經上説：「西方山中有蛇，頭尾差大，有色五彩，人物觸之者，中頭則尾至；中尾則頭至，名曰率然，會稽常山最多此蛇。」

WAGE WAR LIKE A SERPENT

AN ABLE MILITARY COMMANDER IS LIKE THE SHUAIRAN SNAKE OF CHANG MOUNTAIN ...

IF YOU ATTACK ITS HEAD, ITS TAIL STRIKES:

IF YOU ATTACK ITS TAIL, ITS HEAD STRIKES:

IF YOU ATTACK ITS MIDDLE, BOTH ITS HEAD AND TAIL STRIKE.

CAN AN ARMY FIGHT LIKE THIS?

CERTAINLY.

FOR INSTANCE, SUPPOSE THERE WERE TWO MEN, ONE FROM WU AND ONE FROM YUE, WHO WERE ENEMIES ...

NOW, IF THEY HAPPENED TO BE ON THE SAME BOAT IN THE EVENT OF A TERRIBLE STORM, THEY WOULD BECOME LIKE THE LEFT AND RIGHT HANDS OF THE SAME PERSON, HELPING EACH OTHER OUT OF DIFFICULTY.

SO, EVEN STRINGING THE HORSES TOGETHER, BURYING THE CHARIOT WHEELS IN THE DIRT, AND FORCING THE SOLDIERS TO MARCH IN UNISON CANNOT BE COUNTED ON TO CREATE COOPERATION AMONG THE SOLDIERS.

YOU MUST ENCOURAGE THE SOLDIERS TO FIGHT WITH BRAVERY AND UNITY, GIVE THEM THE DISCIPLINE TO FOLLOW COMMANDS, AND MAKE BOTH THE STRONG AND WEAK GIVE THEIR ALL.

YOU MUST ALSO UNDERSTAND GEOGRAPHICAL CONDITIONS AND USE THEM TO YOUR ADVANTAGE.

吳、越是世仇，孫子舉吳人和越人同乘一船而遇風浪時，彼此非互相幫助不可的例子，目的在說明士卒在不得已的境地時，非奮戰不可的道理。

123

「九地」之中，孫子最重視「死地」，他除說「死地則戰」的話外，還一再強調「投之亡地然後存，陷之死地然後生」，以及「死地，吾將示之以不活。」這些都是針對士卒的心理而發。不過「置之死地而後生」並非用兵常道，不得已而用之，不能以常法視之。

FOR AN ABLE MILITARY COMMANDER, DIRECTING THE OPERATIONS OF AN ENTIRE ARMY IS AS EASY AS DIRECTING THE ACTIONS OF A SINGLE PERSON....

TO THE DEATH.

THERE'S NO RETREAT ...

BECAUSE HE PUTS THE SOLDIERS IN A SITUATION WHERE THEY ARE FORCED TO FIGHT.

THE GREAT COMMANDER OF A LARGE FORCE IS ABLE TO RALLY HIS SOLDIERS TO ACT WITH ONE MIND, GOING THROUGH THICK AND THIN AND HELPING EACH OTHER OUT OF TROUBLE. HE DOES THIS BY PLACING THEM ON "MORTAL GROUND," THUS GIVING THEM NO CHOICE BUT TO FIGHT OR DIE.

CHAPTER 12

INCENDIARY WARFARE

火攻主要說明「以火助攻」的方法，古代作戰的防禦工事多以木、竹、籐、革等材料為主，易於引火燃燒，因此火攻就是一項有力的武器，如果各方面配合得宜，往往可以一舉殲敵，所以孫子專列一章「火攻」，來說明「火力」之運用。

施行火攻必須具備一定的條件，同時引火的工具也要經常準備，時機上要選擇天氣乾燥，久旱不雨的季節。另外還要注意起風的日期，當月亮與二十八宿中箕、壁、翼、軫四宿成一線時，就是起風的日子，所以火攻運用必略知天象不可。

孫子由「火攻」說到用兵之是否合於國家利益之大前提，這是頗有感慨之言。因為國君和將帥一怒而興兵，其後果往往和一場大火後的劫難一樣，火焚萬戶不過頃刻之間的事，而重建恢復，則需極長的時間，因此國君和將帥在興兵前，必須先考慮是否合於國家利益。

「用間」是孫子兵法最末一篇，「始計」是對戰爭的通盤考慮估算，所以放在最前面，「用間」是知敵察敵的手段，也是致勝關鍵，所以放在最後。

孫子認為：「不知敵之情者，不仁之至也。」是強調情報工作之重要性，如果因不知敵情而失敗，則一切努力白費外，還白白犧牲人民的生命財產，所以孫子要批評為「不仁」了。

CHAPTER 13

ESPIONAGE

「用間」主要說明運用間諜，達到知敵察敵的目的。以舉國之力，爭勝負於疆場。這是國家人民安危之所繫，因此敵人之一舉一動都應詳為偵察，所以派間諜探敵情實為用兵克敵不可缺少的一環。

正確的情報工作，做為將帥用兵的研判資料，毫不渗入迷信的色彩，的確難能可貴。

孫子兵法最可貴的是具備科學的精神，在二千五百年前的時代，孫子能不宥於占卜星象，強調以具體

132

THE FIVE SPIES

THERE ARE FIVE KINDS OF ESPIONAGE:
- VILLAGE ESPIONAGE
- INTERNAL ESPIONAGE
- DOUBLE ESPIONAGE
- EXPENDABLE ESPIONAGE
- LIVING ESPIONAGE

WHEN THESE FIVE KINDS OF AGENTS ARE USED TOGETHER, THEY WILL BE UNFATHOMABLE TO THE ENEMY, AND THE RESULTS WILL BE MIRACULOUS. THEY ARE NATIONAL TREASURES.

"VILLAGE ESPIONAGE" REFERS TO USING A VILLAGER IN THE ENEMY COUNTRY AS ONE'S SPY.

"INTERNAL ESPIONAGE" REFERS TO USING A MINISTER OF THE ENEMY GOVERNMENT AS A SPY.

「鄉間」和「內間」都是利用敵國的人民或官吏做間諜，孫子說：「鄉間者，因其鄉人而用之；內間者，因其官人而用之。」不過間諜人選的產生，並非易事，而且有時需付出大的代價才能收買敵國的人民或官吏當間諜。

133

孫子在「五間」之中，特別重視「反間」，認為「五間之事，主必知之，知之必在於反間。」就現代眼光來看，「反間」之運用之道，也可視之為反情報的工作範圍，如「必索敵間之來間我者。」其實就是保密防諜的反制技巧。

ONLY AN EXTREMELY CLEVER COMMANDER CAN USE SPIES PROPERLY.

ONLY A BENEVOLENT AND RIGHTEOUS MAN IS ABLE TO DISPATCH SPIES.

ONLY A MAN WITH CAREFUL AND CLEVER MEANS CAN TELL IF A SPY'S REPORT IS TRUE OR NOT.

WONDERFUL! SIMPLY WONDERFUL! A SPY CAN BE USED ANYWHERE.

HOWEVER, IF AN ESPIONAGE OPERATION IS EXPOSED, BOTH THE SPY AND THE PERSON WHO EXPOSED HIM MUST DIE.

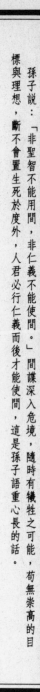

孫子說：「非聖智不能用間，非仁義不能使間。」間諜深入危境，隨時有犧牲之可能，人君必行仁義而後才能使間，這是孫子語重心長的話。苟無崇高的目標與理想，斷不會置生死於度外，

間諜所擔任的工作是情報的蒐集、分析、研判工作，所以舉凡軍旅所至的地區目標情況，守將習性，甚至其左右人士，門房侍衛都要弄清楚，這種嚴密的情報資料蒐集，當然可以幫助將帥瞭解敵情。

WHETHER YOU WANT TO ATTACK A CERTAIN PLACE, LAY SIEGE TO A CITY, OR ASSASSINATE AN ENEMY GENERAL, YOU MUST FIRST HAVE A SPY FIND OUT THE NAME AND CHARACTER OF THE COMMANDER IN CHARGE, HIS ADVISERS, HIS SECRETARY, HIS GUARDS, AND HIS ATTENDANTS.

EVEN MORE IMPORTANTLY, YOU MUST FIND OUT WHO THE ENEMY'S SPIES ARE AND TRY TO BUY THEM OVER TO YOUR SIDE.

USE THE HELP OF THE DOUBLE AGENT TO CULTIVATE THE ASSISTANCE OF VILLAGE AGENTS AND INTERNAL AGENTS. THEN USE THE EXPENDABLE AGENT TO FOOL THE ENEMY AND, FINALLY, USE THE LIVING AGENT TO FIND OUT WHAT THE ENEMY'S PLANS ARE.

IN USING THESE FIVE KINDS OF AGENTS, THE KING SHOULD UNDERSTAND THAT THE KEY TO THEIR SUCCESS IS THE DOUBLE AGENT.

THEREFORE, YOU MUST CERTAINLY GIVE VERY SPECIAL TREATMENT TO THE DOUBLE AGENT.

IN THE PAST, THE REASON FOR THE RISE OF THE SHANG DYNASTY WAS THAT YI YIN HAD BEEN A MINISTER FOR THE PRECEDING XIA DYNASTY.

THE REASON FOR THE RISE OF THE ZHOU DYNASTY WAS THAT JIANG SHANG HAD BEEN A MINISTER FOR THE PRECEDING SHANG DYNASTY.

SO WE CAN SEE THAT FOR AN INTELLIGENT KING AND GENERAL TO EFFECTIVELY EMPLOY WISE AND ABLE PEOPLE AS SPIES WILL BRING CERTAIN SUCCESS.

THIS IS THE ESSENTIAL FIRST STEP OF ANY MILITARY CAMPAIGN. THE ENTIRE ARMY DEPENDS ON THE INFORMATION PROVIDED THROUGH ESPIONAGE AND CANNOT MOVE WITHOUT IT.

近代對「情報」二字的定義有：「情報即知識」、「情報即智慧」的說法，可見情報工作非大智之士不能擔任，所以孫子說「間必上智」、「能以上智為間、必成大功」，這是因為整個軍旅的行動都靠著情報工作是否正確而後才行動的道理。

137

Guide to Pronunciation

There are different systems of Romanization of Chinese words, but in all of these systems the sounds of the letters used do not necessarily correspond to those sounds which we are accustomed to using in English (for instance, would you have guessed that *zh* is pronounced like *j*?). Of course, these systems can be learned, but to save some time and effort for the reader who is not a student of Chinese, we have provided the following pronunciation guide. The Chinese words appear on the left as they do in the text and are followed by their pronunciations. Just sound out the pronunciations as you would an unfamiliar English word, and you will be quite close to the proper Mandarin pronunciation.

Notes:

    -dz is a combination of a *d* and a *z* in one sound, without the *ee* sound at the end, so it sounds kind of like a bee in flight with a slight *d* sound at the beginning.

    -ew is pronounced like the *ew* in *few*.

Bingfa: beeng-fa (*a* as in father)

Chang: chong
Chu: choo

Dao: dow

Helü: hu(*u* as in pull)-lew

Jiang Shang: jyong shong
Jin: jeen

Kongzi: kong (long o)-dz

Mengzi: mung-dz

Qi: chee

Shang: shong
Shuairan: shry-ron
Sun Wu: swoon (*oo* as in b*oo*k)-oo
Sunzi: swoon (*oo* as in b*oo*k)-dz

Wu: oo

Xia: shyaw

Yi Yin: ee-een
Ying: eeng
Yue: yweh

Zhou: joe
Zhuangzi: jwong-dz
Zi: dz